Benazir Bhutto

Benazir Bhutto

Sean Stewart Price

Heinemann Library
Chicago, IL

www.heinemannraintree.com
Visit our website to find out
more information about
Heinemann-Raintree books.

To order:
☎ Phone 888-454-2279
🖥 Visit www.heinemannraintree.com
to browse our catalog and order online.

Edited by Adam Miller, Andrew Farrow, and Adrian Vigliano
Designed by Kimberly R. Miracle and Betsy Wernert
Original illustrations © Capstone Global Library, LLC
Illustrated by Mapping Specialists
Picture research by Ruth Blair
Originated by Heinemann Library
Printed in the United States by Corporate Graphics

14 13 12 11 10
10 9 8 7 6 5 4 3 2

Library of Congress Cataloging-in-Publication Data
Price, Sean.
  Benazir Bhutto / Sean Stewart Price.
    p. cm. -- (Front-page lives)
  Includes bibliographical references and index.
  ISBN 978-1-4329-3222-0
1. Bhutto, Benazir--Juvenile literature. 2. Prime ministers-
-Pakistan--Biography--Juvenile literature. 3. Women prime
ministers--Pakistan--Biography--Juvenile literature. 4.
Pakistan--Politics and government--1971-1988--Juvenile
literature. 5. Pakistan--Politics and government--1988---
Juvenile literature. I. Title.
  DS389.22.B48P75 2009
  954.9105'2092--dc22
  [B]
                        2009018315

032010
005708RP

Acknowledgments

The author and publishers are grateful to the following
for permission to reproduce copyright material: Corbis
p.85; Corbis/Bettmann **p.11**; Corbis/Bettmann **p.21**; Corbis/
Bettmann **p.30**; Corbis/Dominique Aubert/Sygma **p.81**;
Corbis/epa **p.43**; Corbis/Peter Turnley **p.59**; Corbis/Reuters
p.45; Getty Images/AFP **p.89**; Getty Images/AFP/Luke Frazza
p.66; Getty Images/Brad Markel **p.71**; Getty Images/Hulton
Archive **p.23**; Getty Images/Hulton Archive **p.33**; Getty
Images/Rolls Press/Popperfoto **p.16**; Getty Images/Time
Life Pictures **p.7**; Getty Images/Time & Life Pictures **p.63**;
PA Photos **p.79**; PA Photos/AP **p.53**; Rex Features **p.57**;
Rex Features/David Hartley **p.92**; Rex Features/Ilyas J Dean
p.76; Rex Features/Sipa Press p.35; Rex Features/Sipa Press
p.49; Shutterstock background images and design features
throughout.

Cover photograph of Benazir Bhutto speaking during a press
conference in Dubai, 17 October 2007 reproduced with
permission of Corbis/Ali Haider/epa.

We would like to thank Elizabeth Chacko for her invaluable
help in the preparation of this book.

Table of Contents

Some words are shown in bold, **like this**. You can find out what they mean by looking in the glossary.

Coming to Power

On August 17, 1988, a plane crash turned Benazir Bhutto into a world leader. The plane carried the leader of Pakistan, General Muhammad Zia ul-Haq, and other important people.[1] Nobody knows what caused the crash. But the impact on Pakistan and the world was enormous. General Zia, who had ruled Pakistan with an iron hand since 1977, was dead.

DEMOCRACY IN PAKISTAN

During Zia's 11-year rule, Benazir Bhutto had led a group called the **Pakistan People's Party (PPP)**. She had worked to restore **democracy** in Pakistan. Bhutto's effort was as personal as it was political. Zia had come to power by overthrowing and killing Bhutto's father.

Now that Zia was dead, Bhutto had a real shot at achieving her goal of a democratic Pakistan. She would run for prime minister. The elections were scheduled for November 16, 1988. But the path to the election was full of obstacles. In the first place, the 35-year-old Bhutto was about to give birth to her first child. She was also a woman in a country where women were not traditionally political leaders.

But Bhutto won the election. On December 2, 1988, she was sworn in as the prime minister of Pakistan. She was the first woman to lead a modern **Muslim** country and the youngest head of state in the world at that time. She was also the first person to lead Pakistan through free and fair elections. People celebrated this event joyously.[2]

Benazir Bhutto addresses the crowd at a PPP election rally in Punjab.

"THE PATH OF LOVE"

"We will choose the path of love," Bhutto declared in her first speech
as prime minister. "We will eradicate [eliminate] hunger and poverty.
We will provide shelter for the homeless. We will provide employment
for the unemployed. We will educate the illiterates [people who can't
read and write]." She quickly released thousands of captives from Zia's
prisons. She also lifted **censorship** of the press and allowed people to
assemble and speak.[3]

But Pakistan faced countless pressing problems at this time. The country
had no money. Meanwhile, the Zia **regime** had neglected basic services
like education, health care, and housing. Poor people cried out for help.
What little money the country had was tied up in military spending.
Bhutto could only cut the military budget at the risk of triggering another
military takeover.

As Bhutto became a major force in Pakistan's politics for the next two
decades, many would argue that she failed to achieve many of the goals
she put forth in her early speech. But she was an inspiration to millions,
especially to Muslim women. She championed democracy and freedom
in a country that had seen little of either. And she became a voice for
human rights when others carried out cruelty and **repression**.

Even Bhutto's critics agreed that she was brave. She faced down
assassins and lived for years in prison to keep faith with her followers.
In fact, this commitment to Pakistan would eventually cost
Bhutto her life.

This remarkable woman's story begins in the city of Karachi
in 1953. . . .[4] ❖

HEADLINES: 1953–1968

Here are some major news stories from Benazir Bhutto's childhood.

Saudi Arabia Experiences Its First Oil Boom

Oil was discovered in Saudi Arabia in 1938. But World War II prevented drilling and exploration. With the war over in 1945, the Saudis began tapping into their huge reserves of oil. In the early 1950s, the country experienced its first "oil boom." Billions of dollars suddenly flowed into the country, as the formerly poor Saudis sold their oil throughout the world. This allowed them to build roads, schools, and install electricity in homes. But most Saudis followed a strict version of **Islam** called Wahhabism that rejects many modern ideas. Many Saudis mistrusted or opposed these abrupt changes.

U.S. Tests Hydrogen Bomb

On March 1, 1954, the United States exploded the first hydrogen bomb. The bomb was 1,000 times more powerful than the first wartime atomic bomb dropped on Hiroshima, Japan, just nine years before. The United States and **Soviet Union** were fighting the **Cold War**. Both countries raced to produce more powerful weapons.

Polio Vaccine Saves Millions

In 1955 U.S. doctor Jonas Salk helped invent the world's first vaccine against polio, a disease that killed or crippled thousands each year. A vaccine is a drug that prevents people from getting a disease. Within a decade, the vaccine produced by Salk and another vaccine produced by U.S. researcher Albert Sabin were protecting children worldwide.

Soviets Send *Sputnik 1* into Space

On October 4, 1957, the Soviet Union surprised the world by launching the first human-made satellite into space. The Soviets called their satellite *Sputnik 1*. The "beep-beep-beep" signal from *Sputnik 1* worried Americans. The U.S. government soon began a space program of its own.

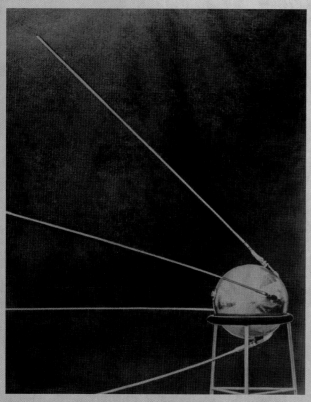

This official photo of the satellite Sputnik 1 *was released by the Soviet government in Moscow. The satellite rests on a stand, and its four antennae can be seen projecting from the main structure of the satellite.*

President Kennedy Assassinated

On November 22, 1963, U.S. President John F. Kennedy was shot by an assassin in Dallas, Texas. The youthful Kennedy's death was a shock to many around the world. A troubled former U.S. marine named Lee Harvey Oswald was arrested as the suspected assassin. Oswald himself was shot by a man named Jack Ruby while in police custody.

The Beatles Arrive in the United States

On February 12, 1964, shrieking teenage girls welcomed the UK's hottest rock group, the Beatles, to New York City. Fans overwhelmed security at the airport while trying to get a glimpse of the four "lads from Liverpool." The group's latest release, "I Want to Hold Your Hand," skyrocketed to the top of the U.S. charts.

Growing Up

Benazir Bhutto was born in Karachi, Pakistan, on June 21, 1953. Her father was named Zulfikar Bhutto. He was a high-ranking government official. Her mother, Nusrat, was from Iran.

Benazir's name means "without comparison." Her skin was unusually rosy for a Pakistani baby, so she was immediately nicknamed "Pinkie." Her family and closest friends called Benazir "Pinkie" for the rest of her life.[1] Benazir was the Bhuttos' oldest child. She had a brother named Mir Murtaza, born in 1954; a sister named Sanam, born in 1957; and another brother, named Shah Nawaz, born in 1958.[2]

At the time of Benazir's birth, Pakistan was a new nation made up mostly of Muslims (see box). Her parents were both Muslims. They followed the religion of Islam. Benazir's father belonged to the Sunni branch of Islam. Like most people in Pakistan, Benazir was brought up as a Sunni. However, her mother belonged to the Shiite branch of Islam. This difference might have been a problem in many Pakistani families. But the Bhuttos were very open-minded. That showed in the way the Bhuttos raised Benazir.[3]

In many Muslim countries, girls are not educated at all. But the four Bhutto children were all raised with the same high expectations, no matter if they were girls or boys. Benazir's father told his children over and over, "I ask only one thing of you, that you do well in your studies."[4]

The formation of Pakistan

In 1947—six years before Benazir's birth—India was a **colony** of Great Britain. But a strong movement in India fought for independence from Britain. The pro-independence forces were split along religious lines. They were dominated by the majority **Hindus**, who were led by Mohandas Gandhi. However, a large minority were Muslims, led by Muhammad Ali Jinnah.

On August 14, 1947, India gained its independence from Britain. Gandhi wanted India to remain united. But Jinnah insisted that Muslims must have their own country, which was to be called Pakistan. The name means "pure land" in Urdu, the national language.[5]

Jinnah and the Muslims got their country. But the India–Pakistan split triggered one of the most grisly bloodbaths in modern history. In majority Muslim areas, Muslims attacked Hindus to drive them out. In majority Hindu areas, Hindus attacked Muslims to drive them out. During 1947 and 1948, at least 500,000 people died in this religious fighting. Another 14 million were driven from their homes. India and Pakistan have been deeply hostile to each other ever since.[6]

FAMOUS FATHER

Zulfikar Bhutto was highly educated. Born in 1928, he had gone to college at the University of California at Berkeley and at Christ Church College at the University of Oxford, in England. He could trace his ancestry back to ancient times. For the last 350 years or so, the Bhuttos have been one of the largest landholding families in the Sindh province, now in southeastern Pakistan (see map on page 15).

> *"I saw my father as much on the front pages of the newspapers as in person."*
> —Benazir Bhutto, recalling her childhood spent with a famous father

Thanks to his great wealth and education, Zulfikar Bhutto became politically powerful as a very young man.[7] In 1957, at age 29, he was appointed to represent Pakistan in the **United Nations (U.N.)** in New York City. It was the first of his many government positions, which included foreign minister and minister of energy. "I saw my father as much on the front pages of the newspapers as in person," Benazir later recalled.[8]

Zulfikar Bhutto traveled a lot throughout the 1950s and 1960s. He often took his wife with him. But the Bhuttos had loyal servants to look after their children. In fact, one of Benazir's first words as a little girl was "enter," the command for bidding a servant into a room.[9]

GOING TO SCHOOL

At the time, most of the top schools in Pakistan were Christian schools. (They could only operate by promising not to convert their Muslim students to Christianity.) Benazir was only three when she began attending the Lady Jennings nursery school. At five, she went to the Convent of Jesus and Mary in Karachi. As she grew older, her parents hired tutors in math and English. Her father would call to check up on his children's schooling, no matter where he was in the world. "Luckily, I was a good student," Benazir later recalled.[10]

As Benazir got older, her mother introduced her to wearing the *burqa*. This is a full-length garment, like a cloak or robe, that hangs over the

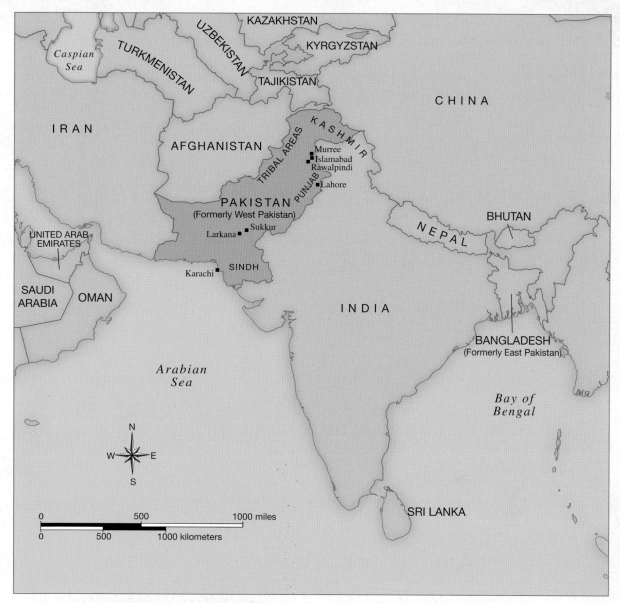

This map shows a broad overview of Pakistan and the neighboring regions. Please refer back to this page as countries are discussed throughout the book.

entire body and sometimes covers the face. Women in many Muslim countries are required to wear *burqas*. But Benazir hated it. She found the *burqa* oppressively hot. When her father found out that Benazir was wearing a *burqa*, he said that she should take it off. Zulfikar felt his daughter should be judged by her character and her mind, not her

September 1972: Benazir Bhutto (far right) on a visit to London, England. She is pictured here with her brother, Murtaza, her mother Nusrat, and the wife of Pakistan's London ambassador, Almas Daul.

clothing. "I became the first Bhutto woman to be released from a life spent in perpetual [never-ending] twilight," Benazir later wrote.[11]

From the time she was very young, Benazir's father tried to engage her in his work. She often traveled with him, meeting important people from other countries. In November 1963, when Benazir was 10, the older Bhutto shook her awake one night. He told her that U.S. President John F. Kennedy had been shot (see page 11). "This is no time to sleep," he told her. Her father had met Kennedy many times and admired him.[12]

SENT AWAY TO SCHOOL

In 1963 Benazir and her sister, Sanam ("Sunny"), were sent to a Catholic boarding school called Murree, located in northern Pakistan. Most of

Pakistan's top families sent their daughters there. This school was a big change for a girl who had been indulged all her life. She had to sleep in a dormitory with 20 other girls. Most shocking of all, there were no servants. "For the first time I had to make my own bed, polish my shoes, carry water for bathing and toothbrushing back and forth from the water taps," Benazir later said. The nuns running the school hit Benazir and Sunny with a brush when they violated the school's strict rules.[13]

WAR OVER KASHMIR

On September 6, 1965, during Benazir's second and final year at Murree, Pakistan went to war once again with neighboring India. They fought over a long-contested region called Kashmir (see below). Murree, which is in the foothills of the Himalaya Mountains, overlooked the Kashmir valley. The school was also on a logical route for an Indian invasion of Pakistan. The girls at Murree had the thrill of practicing air-raid drills and blacking out windows at night. They wondered aloud what it would

Why fight over Kashmir?

One of the ongoing sources of India–Pakistan hostility is the Kashmir region. It is a mountainous region in the north populated by about nine million people today (see map on page 15).

During the 1947 split, most of Kashmir went to India. However, its population is 60 percent Muslim, so Pakistan still claims the area. India and Pakistan have twice gone to war over Kashmir. India says that Pakistan has been training **fundamentalist** Muslims to rebel against existing rulers in Kashmir. Pakistan denies this. Years of **insurgent** attacks and cross-border shootings have killed tens of thousands of people.[14]

be like to be captured by the enemy.[15] But the war ended after just 17 days, and nothing exciting happened at Murree.

The 1965 war over Kashmir would have a big impact on Benazir's life. In peace talks with India, Pakistani President Ayub Khan gave up territory that Pakistan had gained in the war. This disgusted Benazir's father, Zulfikar Bhutto. He resigned from the government in 1966. Sensing Ayub's unpopularity, he set up his own political party, called the Pakistan People's Party (PPP), in 1967.[16]

GROWING ANGER

People were angry with Ayub and the government for many reasons, not just the war. Pakistan had been under Ayub's military rule since he had violently taken over the government in 1958. The country's economy had grown. But most of Pakistan's wealth had gone to just 22 families. These families controlled two-thirds of all industries and four-fifths of all banking and insurance.[17] Most of the country was very poor (see box). Zulfikar Bhutto and the PPP's slogan became "Bread, Clothing, and Shelter." He was a talented speaker who expressed the long-simmering anger of poor people, even though he was wealthy himself. "There is no law of God that we here in Pakistan alone should be poor," he told huge crowds. Benazir, who was then 14 years old, remembered long lines forming outside the gates of her family's house in Karachi each day. These people were waiting to sign up for the PPP.[18]

A DANGEROUS JOB

Ayub first tried to bribe Benazir's father into backing down. When that did not work, he tried death threats. Ayub's supporters repeatedly shot at Zulfikar during political rallies. Each of these attempts failed. But they understandably terrified Benazir. Even so, she hid her fear and tried to be philosophical. "This was the life of politics in Pakistan, and therefore the life we led," she later wrote. "Death threats. Corruption. Violence. What was, was."[19]

> *"This was the life of politics in Pakistan, and therefore the life we led. Death threats. Corruption. Violence. What was, was."*
> —Benazir Bhutto, talking about coming to grips with the dangers facing her family because of her father's political career

In 1968 Ayub had Zulfikar Bhutto arrested. Benazir's father spent time in some of Pakistan's worst, most rat-infested prisons. Even during this time, one of his main concerns was his children's schooling. Benazir had returned to the Convent of Jesus and Mary. She was still only 15, but she was on the verge of completing high school. "I am really proud to have a daughter who is so bright. . . ," her father wrote from prison. "At this rate, you might become president."[20] ❖

Pakistan's poor

Zulfikar Bhutto fought for the poor, but he and his family led a privileged life. Then and now, most Pakistanis do not enjoy such a lifestyle. Pakistan is one of the world's poorest countries. Today, the poorest families live on about $2 a day. There is little privacy for most people in Pakistan. Pakistanis believe in having large families, so their small houses or apartments are usually crowded. Several children often sleep in the same room with their parents.[21]

HEADLINES: 1969–1976

Here are some major news stories from Bhutto's college years.

Anti-War Activists Take over College Campuses

In 1969 U.S. students from New York to California seized college campuses in an effort to protest against the Vietnam War. Students often took over campus buildings and refused to leave, in order to make their point.

Armstrong Becomes First Person to Walk on the Moon

On July 20, 1969, U.S. astronaut Neil Armstrong became the first human to walk on the Moon. Armstrong's landing capped an effort started in 1961 by President John F. Kennedy to send an astronaut to the lunar surface.

Israel and Arab Countries Fight Yom Kippur War

On October 6, 1973, a **coalition** of **Arab** nations, led by Egypt and Syria, launched a surprise attack against Israel. The invasion came on Yom Kippur, a Jewish holiday. The Arab countries did well in the first 48 hours. However, momentum soon swung to the Israelis. The war ended on October 26. The Arab countries were trying to win back lands that they believed were taken by the Israelis from Arab Palestinians.

Oil Embargo Causes Price Shocks

Gasoline prices soared in 1973 after oil-producing countries refused to ship oil to the United States. Oil-rich countries, led by Saudi Arabia, wanted to punish the United States for its support of Israel in the Yom Kippur War. Saudi Arabia is a leader in the Organization of Petroleum Exporting Countries, or OPEC. OPEC's cutback in oil production caused worldwide shortages of gasoline for the first time. The shortages caused gasoline prices to soar.

Watergate Scandal Causes Nixon to Resign

On August 8, 1974, Richard Nixon became the first U.S. president to resign from office. He resigned as a result of the Watergate scandal. This scandal involved a series of crimes carried out by Nixon's 1972 reelection campaign. A group of men working for Nixon, a Republican, were caught breaking into the Watergate Hotel in 1972. They were there to plant listening devices at the Democratic National Committee's headquarters. They could then listen in on the competition's campaign plans.

Chinese Leader Mao Zedong Dies at 82

China's **communist dictator** Mao Zedong died in 1976 at the age of 82. Mao had ruled China since the communists took power in 1949. Millions of people were executed or died of starvation because of Mao's policies.

Nearly a million people attended Mao Zedong's funeral in Beijing, China.

The Happiest Years

In April 1969, Benazir Bhutto got the news that she had been accepted to enter Radcliffe College in Cambridge, Massachusetts. (This school for women later fully became part of Harvard University.) Her father had also been released from prison. His political movement was gaining in popularity among Pakistan's many poor people. As she headed off to college that August, Benazir had every reason to be hopeful about the future.[1]

The seven years Benazir spent in college were the happiest of her life.[2] College was a shock at first, though. Benazir arrived in the United States in 1969. She was only 16. She was so shy around strangers that she could barely look at them. Also, in Pakistan, people dressed formally when they went out. U.S. college students in the 1960s were just the opposite. They typically wore baggy sweatshirts and patched, faded blue jeans. Many of the boys on campus had long hair and shaggy beards. Some students, both boys and girls, openly drank alcohol. Although it was illegal for young people to drink in the United States, drinking was something widely forbidden in Pakistan.[3]

Benazir's mother, Nusrat, stayed in Cambridge for a few weeks to help Benazir get settled. She bought her daughter a complete wardrobe full of traditional Pakistani clothes. But Benazir realized that her Pakistani clothes made her stand out. As soon as her mother left, she went out and

"Never forget that the money it is costing to send you comes from the land, from the people who sweat and toil on those lands."
—Zulfikar Bhutto, telling Benazir to be aware of her good fortune at attending Radcliffe

April 1972: Benazir Bhutto during her time at Radcliffe College.

bought some sweatshirts and jeans. They were practical and allowed her to follow Muslim rules about dressing modestly.[4]

Benazir's father gave her two good-bye presents before she left Pakistan. The first was a beautiful copy of the Koran, the holy book of Muslims. The other was a piece of advice. Zulfikar Bhutto reminded his daughter that she was getting an opportunity that few people in Pakistan would ever have. "Never forget," he told her, "that the money it is costing to send you comes from the land, from the people who sweat and toil on those lands. You will owe a debt to them, a debt you can repay with God's blessing by using your education to better their lives."[5]

FITTING IN

To her surprise, Benazir found that many Americans did not know where Pakistan even was. At first, this bothered her. But then she saw it as a blessing. People who had never heard of Pakistan had also never heard of the Bhuttos. For the first time in her life, she was not famous because of her family. To those around her, she was just an ordinary student named "Pinkie" Bhutto—though some thought she looked like the famous U.S. folk singer Joan Baez.[6]

Benazir could not blend in totally with her U.S. classmates. She had to follow Islamic rules against smoking, dating, and drinking alcohol. But she became extremely fond of (nonalcoholic) apple cider and peppermint-stick ice cream. And she regularly attended rock concerts and parties.[7]

Benazir also became politically active. She worked at the *Harvard Crimson*, the student newspaper. And she joined groups that were interested in expanding women's rights. She also protested against the U.S. war in Vietnam (see box). At the time, the Vietnam War was deeply unpopular on college campuses. Many students thought the U.S. involvement in Vietnam was wrong.[8]

The Vietnam War

From 1965 to 1973, the United States fought a war in the Southeast Asian country of Vietnam. The war there pitted the communist country of North Vietnam against the noncommunist South Vietnam. The U.S. government's goal was to stop the spread of communism to South Vietnam. However, North Vietnam posed no direct threat to the United States. Most of the U.S. soldiers fighting the war had been drafted, or required to serve in the military.

Many young people did not understand why they had to fight and die so far from home. Antiwar protests were especially strong on college campuses. Antiwar protestors even took over college buildings and burned U.S. flags. However, the antiwar movement was controversial. Many other Americans believed that the war in Vietnam was necessary.[9]

SUDDEN CELEBRITY

In the spring of 1971, Benazir suddenly became a campus celebrity at Radcliffe—but for all the wrong reasons. **Civil war** had broken out between West Pakistan and East Pakistan. The West Pakistani army began a brutal campaign of rape, looting, and murder against the East Pakistanis. "Your army is barbaric," other students told Benazir. But Benazir argued with them. She sincerely believed that the horror stories in the press were made up. It was only years later that she sadly realized that they had been true.[10]

In 1971 Benazir accompanied her father to the U.N. in New York City. Zulfikar Bhutto came to urge the U.N. to get India to withdraw from East Pakistan. He also wanted the U.N. to force East Pakistan to remain united with West Pakistan. But it was no use. World opinion had turned against West Pakistan. East Pakistan declared its independence and became Bangladesh.

COMING TO POWER

This national humiliation actually helped the Bhutto family. The crushing defeat in East Pakistan totally discredited the military, which had been running both East and West Pakistan since 1958. Before the war, in 1970, the PPP had won elections in Pakistan's **National Assembly**, the country's lawmaking body. Unlike the military, the PPP had been elected to serve. That made Zulfikar Bhutto the highest-level official who had been elected by the people to rule. He became Pakistan's president on December 20, 1971.[11] (See box on page 29 for more on the structure of Pakistani politics.)

MORE AND MORE FAMOUS

Pinkie Bhutto was no longer just another student at Radcliffe. She was the daughter of the president of Pakistan. Benazir's fame rose even more in June 1972. That was when she accompanied her father to Simla, India, for a high-level meeting with Indian Prime Minister Indira Gandhi.

The talks between Zulfikar Bhutto and Gandhi dragged on for days. The press had little to write about. As a result, many reporters began to follow Benazir around. They wrote about her good looks and fashionable clothes (which had been borrowed from a friend). She was treated like a rock star—the glamorous face of a new generation. Many hoped that this new generation would find peace for both India and Pakistan.[12]

The talks almost broke down. But Zulfikar Bhutto talked Gandhi into giving up territory that Pakistan had lost in the war and in returning the 93,000 Pakistani prisoners of war. This was a huge success that cemented his popularity back home. He was greeted in Pakistan as a hero.[13]

MOVING ON TO OXFORD

Benazir graduated from Radcliffe in 1973 with honors. She had a degree in political science. However, her father had always planned for her to attend the University of Oxford, in England. In fact, all four of his children were enrolled there at birth. Benazir entered Lady Margaret Hall at Oxford in the fall of 1973. Now 20 years old, she was no longer the meek teenager who had gone off to Radcliffe. She was confident and more of a celebrity than ever.[14]

As a graduation present, her father had given her a yellow convertible sports car. Benazir drove it everywhere around Oxford, and it was instantly recognizable. Her friends noticed that there always seemed to be several parking tickets stuck on the windshield.[15]

East and West Pakistan

When Pakistan emerged as a country, it was divided geographically by India. At first East Pakistan and West Pakistan were united by the Muslim faith shared by their people. But West Pakistanis (like the Bhuttos) took almost all the jobs in the army and the government. These West Pakistan officials sold off East Pakistani resources and took all the money made from them. East Pakistan was basically treated as a colony of West Pakistan. East Pakistani anger exploded in 1971. The West Pakistani army tried to brutally put down this rebellion, killing thousands.

India finally stepped in on behalf of the East Pakistanis, who gladly accepted India's help. India's army defeated the West Pakistani force. East Pakistan became the new nation of Bangladesh (see map on page 15).[16]

After three years at Oxford, Benazir earned her second degree—this one in philosophy, politics, and economics. In December 1976, she ran for—and won—the presidency of the Oxford Union Debating Society. Founded in 1823, the Union was one of the most prestigious groups on campus. Benazir had shown that she was a tough debater, and she had served as an officer in the club.

Benazir was the first Asian woman to hold the Oxford Union presidency. Her father was proud that she had won her first political office. "OVERJOYED AT YOUR ELECTION," he wrote to her. Benazir later recalled, "My three-month term as president was to begin in January of 1977. [When] I flew home to Pakistan for the [semester] break, there wasn't a cloud on my horizon."[17] ❖

Pakistani politics

Pakistan's politics are complicated. The people holding high office frequently change. More importantly, the balance of power among the different offices changes as well. The main positions of power are as follows:

President: Pakistan's president is the head of state. That means he or she is the official head of the country. The president's power was originally limited, but that office's power has grown over time. At some points in history, the president has gained the power to dismiss the National Assembly and call for new elections.

Prime minister: The prime minister is the head of government. He or she is the person who actually runs the country and sets official policies. In many ways, the prime minister is more powerful than the president. But at different times, prime ministers have been at the mercy of presidents.

National Assembly: The National Assembly is Pakistan's lawmaking body. It is roughly equivalent to the U.S. Congress. Most assemblies have been narrowly divided between different parties, so they have not been able to pass many laws.

Military: All of Pakistan's governments have been overshadowed by the military. Military leaders have removed elected leaders several times. **Civilian** leaders know that they cannot anger the military without threat of a new takeover. This meddling by the military is one of the chief reasons that Pakistan's political structure has changed so much over time. Each new takeover redistributes power as generals see fit.

HEADLINES: 1977–1979

Here are some major news stories from the time of Bhutto's early political activity.

Elvis Presley Dies at Age 42

On August 16, 1977, millions of fans mourned the death of rock-and-roll icon Elvis Presley, known as "the King." Presley's husky voice and gyrating hips helped make rock popular in the 1950s. He did not invent rock and roll. However, he is given credit for making it nationally popular. His songs were some of the first rock songs played on popular radio stations.

This photo shows the hearse carrying Elvis Presley's casket from his mansion. Thousands of fans gathered to watch from across the street.

Soviet Union Invades Afghanistan

On December 24, 1979, Soviet tanks rolled into Afghanistan (see map on page 15). Soviet leaders ordered the invasion to expand their country's empire. The invasion angered many Muslims around the world. The Soviet government was officially **atheist**. Muslims did not want millions of fellow believers ruled by such a government. Soviet troops fought a brutal war against Muslim fighters, before finally pulling out in 1989. These Muslim fighters were supported in part by the United States, which continued its Cold War against the Soviet Union.

Camp David Talks Bring Peace

Egypt's President Anwar Sadat made history by signing a peace treaty with Israel in March 1979. The two countries had fought off and on over land disputes since Israel was founded in 1947. Egypt and Israel held their peace talks at Camp David, a wooded presidential retreat in Maryland. U.S. President Jimmy Carter hosted the talks.

Under the agreement, Israel gave greater rights to the Palestinians living in areas under Israeli control. Israel also agreed to give up some of the land it had conquered in wars against Egypt. In return, Egypt agreed to recognize Israel as a country and live in peace. The agreement gave hope for a wider peace between Israel, a mostly Jewish country, and its Muslim neighbors. However, other Arab and Muslim countries considered Egypt's treaty with Israel a betrayal.

Iranian Students Storm U.S. Embassy, Take Hostages

On November 4, 1979, Iranian students took over the U.S. embassy in Tehran, taking approximately 70 hostages. An embassy is an official residence of an ambassador from a foreign country. The students had the backing of Iran's supreme leader, the Ayatollah Khomeini. They took the hostages because of long-standing anger at U.S. interference in Iranian affairs. The hostages would remain in captivity for 444 days.

Terrorists Seize Grand Mosque in Saudi Arabia

On November 20, 1979, a group of fundamentalist Muslims seized Saudi Arabia's Grand Mosque. The mosque is Islam's holiest site. The terrorists were angry with the Saudi government. They believed that the Saudi royal family had become too friendly with Western governments. They also believed that the country was becoming too modernized and was violating Islamic laws. Saudi troops retook the mosque after a dramatic two-week battle. As many as 200 people—including many innocent hostages—were killed.

Zia Takes Over

In March 1977, Benazir Bhutto got a visit from an English police officer at Oxford. She was not in trouble with the law. The police were worried about her safety. That very month her father was running for reelection in Pakistan. Opposition to Zulfikar Bhutto had increased. Strikes threatened to paralyze major cities in Pakistan. Muslim religious leaders demanded that he resign. Those leaders hated her father's modern outlook.

The English police warned Benazir. They said she might be killed or kidnapped. From that day on she had to be more careful. She checked her yellow sports car for bombs before she got in. She also varied her schedule, coming and going at unpredictable times. Benazir continued these safety precautions for the rest of her life.[1]

TAINTED VICTORY

Zulfikar Bhutto won a smashing victory on March 7, 1977. The PPP took 68 percent of the popular vote and 77 percent of the seats in the National Assembly. Yet that only made the unrest worse. The opposition party, the **Pakistan National Alliance (PNA)**, claimed that he had won by voter fraud. Historians say there may have been some truth to this. Violent demonstrations rocked Pakistan's major cities for four months.[2]

Zulfikar Bhutto

Zulfikar Bhutto made genuine **reforms** during his five and a half years as Pakistan's leader, in spite of the criticisms against him. He drafted a new constitution that helped organize Pakistan's chaotic government. The constitution created democratic institutions such as a parliament and popular elections. He also opened doors for women. He named many women to government jobs and gave women a better chance of obtaining college degrees. He raised minimum wages and redistributed land. He also tried to strip the richest "22 families" of their wealth to give it to the poor. Zulfikar had the government take over banks, insurance companies, and factories.[3]

Benazir Bhutto in late 1977. She is shown here shortly after her time at the University of Oxford in England.

Despite this victory, many people were unhappy with Zulfikar Bhutto's leadership. Wealthy people hated him. So did conservative Muslim religious leaders, who opposed expanding women's rights.

Zulfikar also made serious mistakes. His policies caused Pakistan's economy to slow down drastically. More disturbingly, he created his own personal police force. This was needed, he argued, to break the power of the army. However, Zulfikar used this force ruthlessly to imprison and attack hundreds of opponents. During her life, Benazir Bhutto refused to ever admit to her father's shortcomings. She remembered—correctly—that he was worshiped by Pakistan's many poor people.[4]

"NOW YOU CAN HELP ME"

Benazir finally returned home from Oxford on June 25, 1977. She and her father had already mapped out her career. At first, she would

Muhammad Zia ul-Haq

Zia, the son of a Muslim prayer leader, was born in 1924. He started his military career in the British colonial army, and he fought for the British in World War II. After Pakistan's independence, he rose through the ranks to general.

But his most dramatic promotion came in 1976. That is when Zulfikar Bhutto promoted him to army chief of staff, over the heads of five senior generals. He probably thought that this would make Zia loyal to him. Zia had seemed a simple man who was more interested in playing golf than hardball politics. But Zia was a genuinely religious man who—like other army officers—feared and distrusted Zulfikar Bhutto's liberal outlook on politics and Islam.[5]

probably work at the U.N. in New York City for a brief time. Then she would return home and work in the foreign service. "Thank God you have completed your education and are home," Zulfikar Bhutto said as he welcomed his daughter. "Now you can help me."[6]

MISJUDGING THE ARMY

The demonstrations had died down by the time Benazir arrived back in Pakistan. Zulfikar Bhutto made some moves to please fundamentalist Muslims in the PNA. He also agreed to hold new elections in October 1977.

September 1986: General Zia ul-Haq at home with his family in Rawalpindi, Pakistan.

But high-ranking men in the army were not impressed. They had come to dislike Zulfikar's liberal policies. They also felt their troops spent too much time breaking up anti-Bhutto strikes or riots. More importantly, they feared that Zulfikar, despite his talk of democracy, planned to rule Pakistan for life. Many historians agree that this was his plan.

Zulfikar had named General Muhammad Zia ul-Haq (see box on page 34) as his chief of staff in 1976. He thought that this would keep Zia loyal to him. That miscalculation would soon cost him his life.[7]

A TERRIBLE DAY

Early on the morning of July 5, 1977, Benazir was roused abruptly out of bed. "Wake up! Get dressed! Hurry!" her mother called out. "The army's taken over! The army's taken over!"

Zulfikar Bhutto tried to call people to find out what was going on. One of his first calls was to Zia. The general bluntly confirmed that he was taking over the government. But he said he planned to hold new elections within 90 days. "You'll be elected prime minister again, of course, sir, and I'll be saluting you," Zia said.

Then Zia's men cut the phone line. They did not want Zulfikar calling around to rally his supporters. Zia also did not want him to call loyal army troops who might stop the takeover.

Benazir tried to be optimistic. Perhaps Zia meant what he said about holding new elections, she thought. "Don't be an idiot, Pinkie," Zulfikar told his daughter quietly. "Armies do not take over power to relinquish it [give it up]. Nor do generals commit high treason [overthrowing a leader] in order to hold elections and restore democratic constitutions."[8]

UNDER ARREST

Zulfikar Bhutto was taken and put under "protective custody" at a house in Murree. Zia released him three weeks after his arrest. Massive crowds gathered to greet the overthrown leader. Benazir believed that her father's tremendous popularity would save him—perhaps even return him to power. But the Bhuttos soon got word about Zia's plan. He intended to put Zulfikar Bhutto on trial. Zulfikar would face a charge of murdering a political opponent.

The following three months turned into a series of arrests and releases for all the Bhuttos. The most important arrest came on September 17, 1977. Zia's troops hauled away Zulfikar Bhutto in the dead of night. He would spend the rest of his life in prison. After this, Bhutto ordered all of his children to flee overseas for safety. Only Benazir refused to go.[9]

Zia still pretended that the elections he promised would go forward. Benazir remained cautious but hopeful that he might keep his word. It was up to her and her mother to keep the PPP's campaign going. Benazir had spoken before small, polite crowds at the Oxford Union. But her first political speech in Faisalabad was much larger. "Stretching in front of me now in a sports field was a mass of humanity with no boundaries," she later recalled.[10]

---

*"From that moment, I knew
there were no more laws."*
—Benazir Bhutto, recalling the period when
General Zia canceled future elections

Meanwhile, Zia promoted the PNA candidates. But public sympathy for the Bhuttos and the PPP was too strong. It became clear that the PPP would probably win the popular vote. So after Benazir's third speech, Zia had her put under house arrest. The next day, September 30, 1977, he went on television and announced that the elections had been canceled. "From that moment," Benazir wrote, "I knew there were no more laws."[11]

A DIFFICULT TIME

The next year and a half were very difficult for Benazir. Her father's murder trial began on October 24, 1977. It lasted five months. The specific charges against Zulfikar Bhutto may or may not have been true. But there was little doubt that he had threatened and even ordered the murders of political opponents during his rule. Few were surprised when the court handed down a guilty verdict on March 18, 1978. Zulfikar and four codefendants were sentenced to hanging.[12]

Benazir's father appealed to higher courts. But Zia always made sure that the courts were stacked against him. At the same time, harassment against Benazir and her mother increased. On December 17, 1977, the police stormed a cricket match that Benazir and her mother were attending. They **tear-gassed** the crowd, and Nusrat Bhutto received a serious gash in her head that required stitches.[13]

MARTIAL LAW

Zia controlled the press, and so newspapers spread negative stories about Zulfikar Bhutto. They accused him of being a bad Muslim and of government corruption. Benazir and others in the PPP tried to disprove these stories. But opposing Zia's regime grew increasingly dangerous. Under his **martial law**, any type of political activity would be punished harshly. Opponents might be publicly whipped or sent to torture chambers.[14]

Other countries condemned Zia's brutal crackdown. They also criticized the guilty verdict against Zulfikar Bhutto. Dozens of countries called for the death sentence to be changed to life in prison. Countries as different as the Soviet Union, the United States, China, Turkey, Canada, France, and Saudi Arabia asked Zia to show mercy. Even Pakistan's own Supreme Court recommended changing the death sentence to life in prison. All this made Benazir hopeful.[15]

But the final decision remained with Zia. He dashed Benazir's last hopes on April 3, 1979. Jailers abruptly rushed her and her mother to Zulfikar Bhutto's jail cell.

SAYING GOOD-BYE

The cell was damp and searingly hot. The normally plump, well-dressed Zulfikar was a shadow of his former self. He had wasted away from disease and starvation.[16] His clothes were dirty. With no shaving razor, his usually smooth face was full of stubble.

The light in the cell was dim. The jailers refused to open the door, so Benazir could not hug her father one last time. The jailers also refused to give the Bhuttos any privacy. So they spoke in whispers. They were given only a half-hour to say good-bye.

Zulfikar urged Nusrat and Benazir to leave the country. But both of them refused. They felt a duty to keep up the work of the PPP. Benazir's father tried to reassure them both. "Tonight I will be free," he told them. "I will be joining my mother, my father. I am going back to the land of my ancestors in Larkana to become part of its soil, its scent, its air. There will be songs about me. I will become part of its legend."

Almost as soon as he said this, the jailers forced Benazir and her mother to leave. Benazir wanted to sob, but refused to show such weakness in front of her father's executioners. "All I could think of was my head," she recalled later. "'Keep it high,' I told myself. 'They are all watching.'" Fourteen hours later, at 2:04 A.M. on April 4, 1979, Zulfikar Bhutto was hanged. Benazir later swore that at that moment she shot up in bed, feeling the noose around her own neck.[17]

CANCELED ELECTIONS

Early on, it appeared that Zia might yet honor his promise to hold new elections. In September 1979, he had allowed some local elections. But Benazir, now age 26, led the PPP so well that he promptly canceled national elections.[18]

THE INVASION OF AFGHANISTAN

If events had unfolded differently, Zia's regime might have fallen quickly. But events outside of Pakistan saved him. On December 24, 1979, the Soviet Union invaded nearby Afghanistan. The Soviets thought that weak little Afghanistan would be an easy conquest. But the move outraged Muslims around the world. They did not want the Soviet Union, an officially atheist country, ruling over Afghanistan's Muslims. Muslims in Afghanistan felt the same way, and they fought back against the Soviets.

At that time, the Soviet Union was fighting the Cold War against the United States. The United States saw the war in Afghanistan as an opportunity to hurt the Soviets. The United States had earlier cut off aid to Pakistan because of its nuclear program (see box on page 83). But President Ronald Reagan suddenly needed Zia. This was because Pakistan shared a long border with Afghanistan (see map on page 15). Pakistan was the best way to get arms and supplies to Afghan freedom fighters, known as the *mujahideen*.

The United States abruptly became Zia's close ally. Pakistan received $3.2 billion in aid. Americans also sold him state-of-the-art F-16 fighter planes. At the same time, tens of thousands of Afghans fled the fighting in their homeland, winding up in refugee camps in Pakistan. Aid poured in from other countries to help the refugees. Huge amounts of this military and relief money wound up in the pockets of Zia and his officials.[19]

Awash in money, Zia tried to buy off the opposition. He offered bribes to high-ranking PPP officials to join him. They refused. Even so, **corruption** rose sharply during Zia's regime. Widespread corruption coupled with human rights abuses weakened Zia's position. Zia imposed strict Islamic laws. For instance, he made a woman's testimony in court equal to only half that of a man's testimony. Yet even the Muslim hardliners in the PNA, the party that had helped bring down Zulfikar Bhutto, began to turn on Zia because he was so repressive.[20] Benazir Bhutto's time was coming. ❖

The *mujahideen* and Osama bin Laden

The dramatic events of 1979 had a profound and formative effect on Osama bin Laden. Only 21 years old when the Soviet Union invaded Afghanistan, bin Laden had spent much of his life focusing on other issues in his home country of Saudi Arabia. However, when the Soviets invaded, bin Laden's attention was captured, along with most people in the Middle East.

News quickly spread that thousands of refugees were fleeing Afghanistan, pouring into neighboring Pakistan. Most of them were caught in refugee camps, where they had little food, water, or shelter. Though young, bin Laden was from a highly influential Saudi family, and had many resources. He became angry at the reports of his Afghan neighbors being displaced by the Soviets. Within days of the invasion, he traveled to Afghanistan in the hope of finding a way to help his fellow Muslims.

At first bin Laden worked as an extension of the Saudi government, helping to raise funds for the Afghans. Around this time, the United States and Saudi governments began giving money to the Afghan cause, often through Zia's government in Pakistan. These efforts included secretly funding Afghan freedom fighters called the *mujahideen*.

As the Soviet occupation dragged on, bin Laden became increasingly involved with the *mujahideen* as a fighter, as well as a fundraiser. He became well-known as a hero in 1987 during a series of battles in the Afghan mountains. At this point, the tide of the fighting had begun to turn in favor of the Afghan forces. The Soviets would begin leaving Afghanistan in 1988, with all troops fully withdrawn by February 15, 1989.

HEADLINES: 1980–1983

Here are some major news stories from Bhutto's time in prison and under house arrest.

War Breaks out Between Iran and Iraq

On September 22, 1980, three weeks of border clashes erupted into all-out war between Iran and Iraq (see map on page 15). Iraq's superior military gave it the upper hand at first. But Iran fought back fiercely and even occupied Iraqi territory in 1984 and 1986. Both sides finally agreed to a U.N. ceasefire in August 1988. The war killed at least 400,000 people and wounded 750,000 more.

Reagan Elected U.S. President, Becomes Partner with Thatcher

On November 4, 1980, former movie star and California governor Ronald Reagan was elected U.S. president. Reagan came into office promising a more conservative government. He wanted to cut taxes and reduce the role of government. He became a close partner of British Prime Minister Margaret Thatcher. She shared Reagan's economic views. Both leaders also strongly opposed the communist policies of the Soviet Union.

Gunman Wounds Pope in Assassination Attempt

On May 13, 1981, Pope John Paul II was the victim of an assassination attempt. The attempt failed, though John Paul was badly injured. The Turkish assassin was caught and imprisoned.

Pope John Paul II collapses after being shot four times. He had been circling and blessing the crowd of about 20,000 in St. Peter's Square in Rome.

Prince Charles Marries Lady Di

On July 29, 1981, Prince Charles, the heir to the British throne, married Lady Diana Spencer in what was widely described as a "fairy tale" wedding. About 750 million people worldwide watched the ceremony on television. A crowd of 600,000 turned out to greet the newlyweds. The royal marriage produced two sons, but the couple divorced in 1996.

Years of Suffering

The next five years would be the most difficult of Benazir Bhutto's life. She spent most of this time either in prison or under house arrest. Her family was scattered and harassed by Zia's government. Members of the PPP were arrested, tortured, and even killed. Only the idea of continuing her father's work kept Bhutto going. She later said of this period: "Suddenly, I was thrust onto a stage where life became stranger than fiction. My life became so bizarre. In a sense, it was larger than life."[1]

OPPOSING ZIA

In the fall of 1980, the PNA proposed working with the PPP to remove Zia. Bhutto was offended by the idea because of the PNA's history against her father. But her mother, Nusrat Bhutto, saw it as an opportunity. For five months, the PPP, the PNA, and eight other parties formed the Movement to Restore Democracy (MRD). On February 21, 1981, Zia arrested 87 leaders of the MRD, including Nusrat Bhutto. This triggered anti-Zia riots and demonstrations.[2]

But it caused a more important reaction. Benazir's two brothers had left Pakistan shortly after their father's arrest. They both believed that the best way to attack Zia was through acts of terrorism. They formed a group called Al-Zulfiqar, or the Pakistan Liberation Army. On March 2,

1981, hijackers working for the group ordered a Pakistani International Airlines plane to land in Kabul, Afghanistan. They shot and killed a Pakistani diplomat and forced Zia to release 55 political prisoners to Syria.[3]

Pakistani police stand guard at the central jail in Karachi, where Benazir Bhutto was held before being sent to solitary confinement in Sukkur.

CRACKDOWN

These acts of terrorism only angered Zia. He ordered a massive crackdown against all opponents of his regime. Benazir Bhutto was one of about 6,000 people who were arrested. Before, she had always been put under house arrest, usually at the family home in Karachi or their country estate in Larkana, Al-Murtaza. This time she was sent first to jail in Karachi and then to **solitary confinement** in Sukkur. Zia wanted her to confess that she was part of her brothers' terrorist activities.[4]

Bhutto remained in solitary confinement from March to August 1981. Sukkur Jail is a huge brick building in the Sindh desert. Temperatures there can reach 120°F (49°C). Bhutto would always remember this as her worst imprisonment. The water was a dingy yellow. She slept on a rope cot. Insects flew and crawled all over her cell.[5]

Despite all this, Bhutto was lucky. Many PPP supporters had it worse. They were starved for days, beaten with rods, stuck in cramped cells, and had toenails pulled out. Many women were raped. The police wanted them to confess that Benazir Bhutto and her mother were terrorists.[6]

STRANGE REPRIEVE

Strangely, the police interrupted Bhutto's solitary confinement. For two days in September 1981, they let her attend her sister's wedding. This brief break was much needed. Bhutto was able to take a hot bath and sleep on a real bed. More importantly, she found out that an old Cambridge friend named Peter Galbraith was trying to help her. He now worked for the U.S. Senate Committee on Foreign Relations. Even so, she was thrown right back into jail.[7]

HOUSE ARREST

Finally, on December 27, 1981, Bhutto was released from jail and taken to her family's country house in Larkana under house arrest. Only her mother and her sister were allowed to visit. Her mother had endured long months of imprisonment as well, and her health had suffered. At first, doctors thought that she had tuberculosis, a lung disease. But doctors soon discovered that it was lung cancer.

Human rights groups and other governments asked Zia to allow Nusrat Bhutto to leave Pakistan. She could not get the medical care she needed there. For months, Zia denied that she was really ill. Finally, in November 1982, a medical review board reluctantly allowed her to leave the country to seek medical help.

But by then, Benazir Bhutto had health problems of her own. Not long after her father's death, Bhutto began hearing a clicking sound in her ear. The condition had gotten better at times, but had never entirely gone away. It caused pain and swelling in her head and eventually upset her balance (which is controlled by the inner ear). Throughout 1983 the condition worsened. It became clear that, like her mother, she needed better medical care than she could get in Pakistan.[8]

Bhutto was reluctant to leave, even if it was for a good reason. She might not be allowed to come back. What kind of signal would this send to the PPP members? How could she fight for her father's cause overseas? But she was clearly having trouble with her balance, and doctors told her that she might soon lose her hearing. Finally, on January 10, 1984, Bhutto was allowed to leave to seek medical help.[9] ❖

HEADLINES: 1984–1987

Here are some major news stories from Bhutto's time in exile.

Personal Computers Become a Fad

The spread of personal computers began in the mid-1970s. But the introduction of newer, faster computers in the early 1980s caused an explosion in personal computer sales. Many of these computers were made by Apple, which introduced the first Macintosh computers on January 24, 1984. The "Mac" was the first computer to use a "mouse."

Movie Star Rock Hudson Dies of AIDS

On October 2, 1985, many people were shocked to find that actor Rock Hudson had died of a disease called AIDS (short for "acquired immunodeficiency syndrome"). AIDS was new to most people and poorly understood. The death of Hudson, one of Hollywood's most famous leading men, helped to raise the profile of this serious disease.

Coke's New Formula Bombs

In 1985 Coca-Cola changed the formula of its popular soft drink, calling it New Coke. After just two months, New Coke bombed. Few people liked it. The company had to bring back its old formula, calling it Coca-Cola Classic.

Space Shuttle *Challenger* Explodes Shortly after Takeoff

On January 31, 1986, a horrified world watched as the space shuttle *Challenger* exploded shortly after takeoff. The *Challenger* disaster put the U.S. space program on hold for several years. Investigations later showed that technical problems and human error caused the explosion.

Corazon Aquino Replaces Dictator Marcos

In 1986 Filipinos elected Corazon Aquino as their new president. She replaced dictator Ferdinand Marcos, who had ruled the country for 20 years. Aquino's long struggle against a corrupt dictator was frequently compared to Benazir Bhutto's struggle in Pakistan.

Chernobyl Accident Spreads Radiation across Eastern Europe

On April 26, 1986, an accidental explosion at the Soviet Union's Chernobyl nuclear power plant caused thousands of people to flee the area. It was the worst nuclear power plant mishap in history. The accident may have been responsible for as many as 4,000 deaths.

In the aftermath of the Chernobyl disaster, a masked worker examines radiation levels with a Geiger counter.

Exile and Return

Benazir Bhutto originally planned to return to Pakistan soon after the operation on her ear. She felt that even in prison she could rally people against the Zia regime.

But a quick return to Pakistan became medically impossible. Bhutto went to London, England, to have the operation performed on her ear in January 1984. She was 30 years old at this time. The surgery was a success. It relieved the swelling. But the recovery was difficult. She could not sit up for very long without feeling dizzy and nauseous. At times, it felt like her head would explode. Even worse, her doctor warned that another round of surgery might be needed in nine months to a year. Without it, she might lose her hearing.[1]

Bhutto also found that her long imprisonment had damaged her mental state. She later wrote:

> I dreaded going out of the [apartment]. Every time I stepped out the front door my stomach, my neck, and my shoulders tensed. I could not walk two steps without turning around to see if I was being followed. After all the years of living alone behind prison walls, even the crowded streets in London seemed threatening. I wasn't used to people, to voices, to noise.[2]

Bhutto found herself fighting off panic attacks while simply walking through a park. She managed to hide her fear and put on a confident face. Yet adjusting to normal life was very difficult. It did not help that Zia's men often did follow her around. They were probably just watching her movements. But there was no way for Bhutto to know when or if they might turn violent. Fortunately, she was usually able to scare them off by calling the English police.[3]

Bhutto accepted that she had to live in **exile**—at least for a while. But she decided to use her time away from Pakistan constructively. She would rebuild the PPP and help those imprisoned by Zia.

WORRYING SIGNS

There were about 378,000 Pakistanis living in England at the time. Many of them had fled from Zia's ruthlessness. Some were PPP party leaders.[4]

But Bhutto saw some worrying signs. Some of the PPP officials were more concerned about preserving their high offices than in helping those back in Pakistan. Also, most of them were older men. They had a hard time following a 30-year-old woman. In Pakistan's culture, women were considered by most to be inferior to men. However, PPP members had no choice. Bhutto had become the party's leader. The publicity surrounding her imprisonment had made her a huge celebrity.[5]

PUTTING PRESSURE ON ZIA

During the mid-1980s, Bhutto worked tirelessly to publicize Zia's abuses. She traveled to Washington, D.C., to gain the support of members of the U.S. Congress. She also spoke at Harvard and before important international groups like the Carnegie Endowment for International Peace. Likewise, she traveled around Europe to publicize the existence of 40,000 political prisoners back in Pakistan. The PPP issued its own magazine, *Amal* (Action). It kept Pakistanis living away from home informed about what was happening in Pakistan. Bhutto also worked with human rights groups like Amnesty International. They could bring attention to those prisoners in the greatest danger.[6]

All this pressure did have an impact on Zia. He had become very dependent on the United States, thanks to all the aid he received (see pages 39 and 40). Without it, his regime would likely topple. So he was sensitive to calls from the U.S. government for greater democracy. In late 1984 and 1985, Zia held two sham elections in which the PPP refused to participate. Bhutto kept up her worldwide publicity campaign. Unfortunately, sometimes Bhutto's speeches on behalf of prisoners backfired. After one speech, Zia had 54 prisoners sentenced to death.[7]

SEEING FAMILY

In July 1985, Bhutto took some time out to see her family. Her mother, brothers, and sister all agreed to meet in southern France. But the Bhutto family celebration was cruelly interrupted. On the night of July 18, 1985, Bhutto's youngest brother, Shah, died under mysterious circumstances in his French apartment. Just 27 years old, he was apparently poisoned. Shah had been arguing with his wife, who was later charged with failing to help someone in need. But who had given him the poison? Many have pointed the finger at Zia's agents.[8]

The Bhuttos wanted to bury Shah in Pakistan, his homeland. But Zia did not want this. He knew that a funeral for any Bhutto would draw massive crowds who were hostile to him. However, Zia also knew that denying such a burial would be very unpopular with ordinary Pakistanis. Zia finally agreed to let Shah be buried at Al-Murtaza, the family estate in Larkana. Al-Murtaza was far from any city. He thought it would be difficult for large groups to congregate there.

Zia was wrong. About 10,000 people defied roadblocks to greet Benazir Bhutto at the airport on August 21, 1985. At least another 40,000 people defied government barricades to be at the burial. The outpouring of grief was so huge that it forced Zia to finally declare an end to martial law. But that was more a publicity stunt than anything else. It changed nothing. Zia remained in complete control.[9]

> *"Do you want freedom?*
> *Do you want democracy?*
> *Do you want revolution?"*
> —Benazir Bhutto, speaking to
> a large crowd at a rally in 1986

This picture shows the Bhutto family together, many years before the sad event of Shah's death. From left to right are Nusrat, Shah, Zulfikar, and Benazir. Benazir's brother Murtaza is at the bottom left beside her sister Sanam.

PLEDGING TO RETURN

After the funeral, Bhutto told cheering crowds that she would continue to fight for democracy in Pakistan. Zia had promised not to arrest Bhutto. But the size of the crowds and the outpouring of support for Bhutto spooked him. Within less than a week of her return, she was once again under house arrest. She would remain in detention until November. At that point Zia gladly allowed her to return to France. She had to attend the hearings examining her brother's death.[10]

Bhutto pledged to come back soon, and she did. Bhutto's publicity campaign against Zia had worked. Now the whole world was watching this brave young woman as she walked back into the arms of a violent military dictatorship. She practically dared Zia to arrest her again and to crack down on her supporters. If he did, the weight of world public opinion would make him weaker, not stronger.

CHANGES IN FORTUNE

Bhutto's plane arrived in Lahore, Pakistan, on April 10, 1986. At least one million people surrounded the airport to welcome her. Bhutto got in a truck to drive to a rally nearby. But crowds packed the road. They shouted "Long live Bhutto!" while throwing rose petals and garlands of flowers. "The sea of humanity lining the roads, jammed on balconies and roofs, wedged in trees and on lampposts, walking alongside the truck, and stretching back across the fields, was more like an ocean," she later wrote. It took the truck 10 hours to make what was normally a 15-minute drive.[11]

Bhutto was totally exposed to any potential assassin's bullet on the truck. But she felt no danger. "Only someone who was willing to be torn apart by the crowd could harm me," she later said. At the rally, Bhutto could see nothing but people wearing the red, green, and black colors of the PPP.

Bhutto's voice was hoarse because of a bout with the flu. But her concerns about it melted away as she began speaking to the crowd. "Do you want freedom?" she asked the crowd. "Do you want democracy? Do you want revolution?"

"Yes!" the people roared back.

Benazir Bhutto's time had come.[12]

GETTING MARRIED

As Bhutto's fortunes improved, she decided it was time to get married. She wanted a partner, just as most people do. But she also had a political reason. Getting married would make her more attractive to Pakistani voters. It was unusual for a woman to remain unmarried. Starting in 1985, she followed the longstanding tradition of having her family arrange her marriage.

Many of Bhutto's Western friends were surprised that she would consent to an arranged marriage. She later explained that it was the only realistic way she could have a wedding. "It simply would not be possible for me to have a date and get to know a man the way you could," she told a U.S. friend. "Even the hint of a relationship would have been used by my opponents to destroy me politically."[13]

The family of Asif Ali Zardari approached Bhutto's aunt and mother about arranging the marriage. The two had much in common. His father had supported Zulfikar Bhutto. Zardari himself was educated in England. Like Bhutto, he belonged to a powerful landholding family from Sindh province. He helped run his family's construction business.

Bhutto insisted that she keep her own name. She felt that the PPP must be led by someone named Bhutto. Zardari agreed to this, which was unusual for a Pakistani marriage.

A PEOPLE'S WEDDING

The wedding took place on December 19, 1987. More than 100,000 people attended the public reception after the marriage ceremony. A large number of them were reporters. Journalists from Europe, Asia, the United States, and Arab countries like Egypt, as well as Pakistan jostled to get photographs and quotes.

The couple sat on a large stage built specially for the occasion. The event looked more like a rock concert than a wedding. People danced and cheered. Miniature hot-air balloons drifted over the crowd, streaming tails of fire. Car horns blared, occasionally drowning out the popular songs blasting from radios. Fireworks exploded in fountains of silver and gold. "Karachi went wild that night," Bhutto later wrote.

Despite being arranged, the marriage appeared to be a happy one. Getting married made Bhutto more popular than ever.[14] ❖

Benazir Bhutto and Asif Ali Zardari on their wedding day.

Headlines: 1988–1990

Here are some major news stories from the time of Bhutto's first election.

Exxon Valdez Oil Spill Pollutes Alaskan Coastline

On March 24, 1989, the oil tanker *Exxon Valdez* hit a reef off the coast of Alaska and spilled more than 10 million gallons (38 million liters) of crude oil. The oil spill, one of the largest in history, caused an environmental disaster.

Protestors Killed in China's Tiananmen Square

For seven weeks in 1989, pro-democracy protestors took over Tiananmen Square in the heart of Beijing, China. They called for greater openness in China's communist government. But on June 4, the government sent in soldiers, who killed thousands of people and arrested thousands more. The Chinese government crackdown dashed protestors' hopes for a more open society.

Nelson Mandela Released from Prison

On February 11, 1990, South African officials released Nelson Mandela from prison after 27 years. Mandela had been jailed for his opposition to the country's set of laws known as apartheid. These laws separated whites and blacks in all aspects of life and kept black people from enjoying basic freedoms. Later, as South Africa's first black president, he used his position to create unity instead of seeking revenge.

Berlin Wall Falls

On November 9, 1989, Germans celebrated the fall of the Berlin Wall, one of the most hated instruments of communist rule in Eastern Europe. Since 1961 the wall had separated democratic West Germany from communist East Germany. The wall had both symbolic and practical meaning. It was the biggest symbol of the division between the democratic and communist world. It also kept people in the Soviet bloc from traveling wherever they wanted. The wall's collapse was a sign that millions of Europeans would then be free.

A young German man straddles the Berlin Wall and waves victoriously after the fall of communism in Germany.

Hubble Telescope Launched into Space

On April 24, 1990, the United States launched the Hubble Space Telescope into space. The telescope was able to peer deeper into space than any earthbound telescope. It sent back breathtaking photographs of the universe.

Iraq Invades Kuwait

On August 2, 1990, Iraqi dictator Saddam Hussein invaded neighboring Kuwait. The invasion triggered the Gulf War. Led by the United States, dozens of countries helped liberate Kuwait within seven months.

Sudden Victory, Sudden Defeat

Toward the end of his life, Zia said that his greatest mistake was allowing Benazir Bhutto to live.[1] That "mistake" haunted him more and more after Bhutto's return. When Bhutto had left Pakistan in 1984, Zia had held all the power. He had controlled the government with an iron hand. He also had the support of powerful countries such as the United States. Meanwhile, Bhutto had been sick. Her father's political party was in disarray. Most of its leaders were dead, imprisoned, or forced into exile.

But by 1988, the situation had changed radically. Zia's regime was showing signs of strain. Government officials had begun to defy him. Zia said that future elections could not involve political parties. But in 1987, Pakistan's Supreme Court—appointed by Zia— allowed parties. Zia's handpicked prime minister, Mohammad Khan Junejo, also began to defy him. He invited Bhutto to a high-level meeting to discuss the Soviet withdrawal from Afghanistan. This move outraged Zia.[2]

In May 1988, Zia fired Junejo and dismissed the National Assembly, naming himself caretaker president. Zia had promised to call national elections in 1990. But then he moved up the elections to be held in late 1988. What changed his mind? He had found out that Bhutto was pregnant. Her baby would be born at right about the time the elections were held. That would clearly make it difficult for her to campaign.[3]

THE DEATH OF ZIA

Zia's trick might have worked. He might have beaten Bhutto in the election. But an August 18, 1988, plane crash killed him and most of his top generals. People have guessed endlessly about what caused the plane crash that caused Zia's death. Some claim it was caused by enemies. Some people believed that many Pakistanis had motive to remove Zia from power, especially the Bhutto family. Several countries—including the United States, India, Israel, and the Soviet Union—also had motives. But the crash was most likely caused by a mechanical failure.[4]

News of Zia's death triggered widespread celebrations. People honked their car horns and joyfully screamed "Zia is dead!" in the streets. For the first time, people believed that Bhutto and the PPP had a real chance of winning the upcoming elections.[5]

DIVIDED COUNTRY

Not everyone was on the PPP's side. Pakistan was badly split. Death threats had followed Bhutto for years. They became more persistent as the election neared. Also, Bhutto's pregnancy limited her ability to work. At one point she was confined to bed for days in order to protect the baby's health. On September 21, she gave birth to a boy named Bilawal. The name means "one without equal."[6]

Though Zia was dead, his fellow generals were still in power. They had no intention of handing over the government. The caretaker administration insisted that all voters must present official identification (ID) cards. Most PPP supporters were poor and had no ID. This limited the number of them who could vote.[7]

At the same time, violence rocked Pakistan. It was so bad that Bhutto's mother, Nusrat Bhutto, was shot and wounded in early November while campaigning. Many people feared that the violence would cause the military to step in and stop the elections. But the generals who had succeeded Zia refused. Violence or no violence, the elections would go forward.

BECOMING PRIME MINISTER

Bhutto's main opposition came from a group of political parties. They were called the Islamic Democratic Alliance. Bhutto's PPP and the alliance agreed on most issues. Both sides wanted closer ties to the United States and a peaceful nuclear energy program. Both called for support for the Muslim rebels fighting against the Soviet Union in neighboring Afghanistan. And both called for civilian rule with no military interference.

But Bhutto's opponents wanted to make Islam a greater part of people's lives. Most importantly, the alliance leaders wanted Pakistan to follow traditional Islamic laws, called *Sharia*. Bhutto argued for separation of religion and state. Many *Sharia* laws have to do with the way people dress and behave. She feared especially that *Sharia* laws would be used to limit the rights and freedoms of Pakistani women.

Despite these and other obstacles, Bhutto and the PPP won a slim but convincing victory in the November elections. They took 93 of 205 seats in the National Assembly. The PPP joined forces with some smaller parties and formed a majority in the National Assembly. On December 1, 1988, Benazir Bhutto became prime minister. The Zia era was finally over.[8]

INSTANT CELEBRITY

Bhutto's campaign and victory made her an even bigger celebrity in the world press. Television crews swooped in to do interviews. Her face appeared on magazine covers around the globe. Everyone wanted to know how she was challenging the regime that had once imprisoned her. They also wanted to know more about this glamorous new leader.

Though she had lived much of her life in the spotlight, Benazir Bhutto's election as Pakistan's prime minister thrust her toward a new level of worldwide popularity.

Even before the election, she explained her appeal to Pakistan's public to one newspaper like this:

> While women don't generally have rights [in Pakistan], they are looked upon with great respect and a sense of protection. So when there is a sense of tragedy [as there was with her father's execution] there is a sense of 'Let us be the protectors.'. . . Because the people of the country have accepted me, my strength really comes from that.[9]

Bhutto promoted her story by publishing an autobiography called *Daughter of Destiny* (also titled *Daughter of the East*) in 1989.

SET UP TO FAIL

One of Bhutto's first acts as prime minister was to restore democracy. She released political prisoners from Zia's jails and ended censorship of the press. She also ended restrictions on freedom of speech. Student groups, political organizations, and labor unions were no longer banned. Despite tight budgets, the PPP was also able to fund 18,000 more schools and brought electricity to 40,000 villages.[10]

Even with these early successes, Bhutto's government had been set up to fail. Though Zia was dead, the army still meddled in politics. In most Western countries, civilians traditionally control the military. But Pakistan had no such tradition. Under Zia, the army had become a stronghold of fundamentalist Islam. That meant, as a woman, Bhutto got even less respect from top officers than other civilian leaders.

Pakistan's military did a lot to undermine Bhutto's rule. As a condition of taking power, Bhutto had to keep Ghulam Ishaq Khan as president. Ishaq, who was not a PPP member, was close to the military. He also had the power to dismiss the National Assembly at any time. Bhutto had to meet another condition. She had to promise not to cut the defense budget. This kept her from spending money on programs to help the poor.

Women in Pakistan

Zia's "Islamization" policies fell especially hard on women. Pakistani courts used the strictest possible interpretation of *Sharia* laws. This was used to deny women schooling and force them to wear conservative clothing against their will.

The changes were especially harsh when it came to the sensitive crime of rape. Under Zia's laws, it took four male witnesses to back up any woman's accusation of rape. Naturally, this was impossible to achieve. So most rapes went unpunished. Worse, women who accused men of rape were often punished instead. They had, after all, admitted to having sexual relations outside of marriage. By 2003, more than 20,000 women were in prison for "adultery," many of them victims of rape.[11]

Bhutto worked to undo policies like these. She was the mother of two daughters, Bakhtawar (born 1990) and Asifa (born 1993). She wanted them and other women of their generation to have more opportunities. She said, "I want to show [women in Asia] that they can rise above these pressures too, that they can demand to make their own choices, and not have others—fathers, husbands, or brothers—make their choices for them."[12]

But that proved difficult, especially since Bhutto was herself a woman in a political world dominated by men.[13]

FIGHTING FUNDAMENTALISTS

Bhutto had another powerful enemy—the Inter-Services Intelligence (ISI). The ISI is Pakistan's intelligence force, the group in charge of finding information about any enemies to the government. Zia had strengthened the ISI during his reign. By the time Bhutto became prime minister, the ISI was often described as a "government within the government" that was answerable to no one. And it was still loyal to

April 11, 1995: U.S. President Bill Clinton looks on as Benazir Bhutto speaks at a joint press conference in Washington, D.C.

Zia's policy of "Islamization," or making society follow strict Islamic law. ISI agents spied on Bhutto and her supporters. They also gave information about her and the PPP to her opponents.[14]

The ISI turned Pakistan into a home for fundamentalist Muslim terrorists. Between 1979 and 1992, the ISI received billions of dollars from the United States and Saudi Arabia (see pages 39 and 40). This money was supposed to be used to train Islamic fighters to combat communists in Afghanistan. But the ISI used some of the money to build up Muslim terrorist groups to fight the Indians in Kashmir (see box on page 17). The ISI built a series of Muslim schools that taught fundamentalist Islam. Students at these schools later formed the **Taliban**, the fundamentalist Muslim group that later took over Afghanistan.[15]

Bhutto's top civilian opponent was Nawaz Sharif. He was head of a political party called the **Pakistan Muslim League–Nawaz (PML–N)** and had been loyal to Zia. Sharif was also chief minister of Punjab province. As head of the province with the most people, Sharif tried to block any changes that Bhutto made. Sharif and his party also kept up a constant stream of criticism of Bhutto. Bhutto had to spend much of her time and energy responding to these attacks.[16]

RUNNING A RESTLESS COUNTRY

Despite these powerful opponents, Bhutto had strong support among ordinary Pakistanis—at least at first. She came into office making many promises. The rich in Pakistan paid almost no taxes. She wanted to raise taxes on them and lower taxes on the poor. She had also promised to increase funding for education and health care. Women had suffered greatly under Zia (see page 65). Bhutto wanted to change that. She also wanted to give women better opportunities to get jobs and education.

However, Bhutto's majority in the National Assembly was very narrow. Such a narrow majority made it almost impossible to pass new laws. People were glad that democracy had been restored. But they became

Ethnic tensions in Pakistan

Pakistan's population is made up of several different **ethnic groups**—people who have their own language and customs. The major ethnic groups are Punjabi (44.68 percent of the population), Pashtun or Pathan (15.42 percent), Sindhi (14.1 percent), Sariaki (8.38 percent), Mohajir (7.57 percent), Balochi (3.57 percent), and "other" (6.28 percent).[17]

Many of these groups live in separate areas. But in other areas, they live close together. Pakistan's largest city, Karachi, is full of different ethnic groups. One of the largest there is the Mohajirs. These are people who fled India after the 1947 war. They are actually a diverse group of people. But they have one thing in common—they speak Urdu.

Many Mohajirs continued to settle in Karachi. The growing number of Mohajirs was deeply resented by Sindhis and Punjabis. The tensions among these groups boiled over in the mid-1980s during the Zia regime. By the time Bhutto took power, her home province of Sindh was almost in a state of open war. More radical members of each group called for separation from Pakistan. These ethnic tensions would plague Bhutto while in office. They remain a source of violence in Pakistan today.[18]

increasingly restless over time. It became clear that Bhutto and the PPP could not deliver on their promises.[19]

The last straw for Bhutto's government came in 1990. Ethnic violence broke out in Sindh province (see box). The violence escalated to riots and terrorist bombings. More than 500 people were killed. Bhutto tried to use the army to quiet these disturbances. But it did not work.[20]

The army and President Ishaq had planned to remove Bhutto from power as soon as possible. The violence in Sindh province gave them the excuse they needed. In early August, world attention was focused away from Pakistan and on Iraq. On August 2, 1990, Iraq had invaded tiny, oil-rich Kuwait. Four days after that invasion, Ishaq dissolved Pakistan's National Assembly and removed Bhutto from office. She had only served twenty months of her five-year term.[21] ❖

HEADLINES: 1991–1996

Here are some major news stories from the time of Bhutto's second election.

Internet Usage Soars

The Internet is a global system of computer networks that exchanges information. In the 1980s, it was still basically a tool of academics and military experts. In July 1992, a company called Delphi became the first Internet service to offer services like e-mail to the public. Internet usage soon soared. The Internet became a widespread tool for communication and research.

Rwanda Genocide Kills Thousands

For 100 days in 1994, the small African country of Rwanda became a killing field. Tensions between two groups, the Hutus and Tutsis, had always been strong. The Hutu-led government encouraged groups to begin attacking the Tutsis. No Tutsi was safe. Between 500,000 and one million men, women, and children were killed. The United States and European countries did little to stop or slow down the massacres. Tutsi-led rebels finally defeated the Hutu-led government and brought the killing to an end.

Israeli Prime Minister Yitzhak Rabin Assassinated

Hope for peace in the Middle East faded after an Israeli man shot and killed Israeli Prime Minister Yitzhak Rabin on November 4, 1995. The assassin opposed Rabin's efforts to make peace with Palestinians, who had longstanding disputes with Israel. Rabin's death derailed peace talks aimed at ending decades of fighting between Israelis and Palestinians.

Terrorist Attack Rocks Oklahoma City

On April 19, 1995, a truck bomb blew up a U.S. government office building in Oklahoma City, killing 168 and wounding 800. The three bombers were extremely conservative Americans who were angry with the U.S. government.

The terrorist bombing in Oklahoma City left the U.S. in shock, especially after it was discovered that the bombers were U.S. citizens. At the time, this was the worst terrorist attack ever to take place on U.S. soil.

Mad Cow Disease Spreads

In 1996 farmers in the United Kingdom discovered that many of their cattle were infected with mad cow disease. The illness, which can be passed to humans, makes tiny holes in the brain of an affected cow. The brain becomes sponge-like, giving rise to the disease's scientific name, "bovine spongiform encephalopathy," or BSE. Millions of cattle have since had to be destroyed to prevent the spread of the disease to other animals and people.

Prime Minister Again

A new round of elections followed Benazir Bhutto's removal from office in 1990. But her opponents kept her too busy to campaign effectively. They accused her and her husband of corruption. Bhutto's enemies gave her husband, Asif Ali Zardari, the nickname "Mr. Ten Percent." That was the percentage Zardari supposedly asked people to pay him when getting contracts with the Pakistani government. Voters responded by electing Bhutto's main opponent— Nawaz Sharif of the PML–N.[1]

Right away, Sharif began to dismantle many of Bhutto's reforms. He renewed censorship of the press, cracked down on labor unions, and closed many women's health centers. Sharif was a wealthy industrialist. In fact, his family's factories had once been taken by Bhutto's father. He now promoted private business as a way of helping Pakistan's struggling economy.[2]

Sharif also tried to tie Pakistan's laws even more to Islamic *Sharia* laws. However, the PPP and other parties helped block that effort. Sharif had a better relationship with the army than Bhutto, yet he ran into many of the same problems that she had faced. The army and intelligence services simply did not want to give up power to a democratically elected leader.

Like Bhutto, Sharif also failed to stop ethnic fighting in Sindh province (see box on page 68). This helped cause his downfall. The army forced both Sharif and President Ishaq to resign on April 18, 1993. The result was yet another round of elections.[3]

WHIPPING UP SUPPORT

This time Bhutto felt confident about winning. Immediately, she began speaking once again at campaign rallies. Bhutto still had an electric impact on her supporters. As she approached a waiting crowd in a car or truck, waves of people would regularly try to crush in on her. They wanted to touch her or shake her hand. Frequently, her own supporters endangered her life this way. Car horns honked. Men carrying machine guns fired them in the air to celebrate. People showered her path with flower petals and garlands.

The appearance of Bhutto on stage in her trademark white scarf caused the crowd to go wild. Most of the people in her audiences were men. But usually there were some women on the outer fringes. All these supporters clapped and stamped their feet. PPP campaign songs blared from loudspeakers. One of them went:

> Listen, all you holy warriors!
> Look at Benazir, the nation joins her!
> Long live Bhutto! Long live Benazir![4]

ELECTED AGAIN

In 1993 Bhutto was once again elected prime minister. But just barely. The PPP won 86 seats out of 202 in the National Assembly. Bhutto was able to again put together a coalition of small parties. This time her position was strengthened. The new president was Farooq Leghari, a member of the PPP. Bhutto did not have to worry as much about having a hostile president dismiss the National Assembly.

Bhutto's second term began on October 19, 1993. It was more successful than her first. She was able to make the following changes:

- Improve education, open new schools, and reopen women's health clinics

- Expand wireless communication and computer education

- Double tax revenue and triple the national growth rate

- Crack down on kidnappings for ransom, which had become a huge problem in Karachi

- Involve the army and police in international peacekeeping missions.[5]

FAMILY SPLIT

However, these accomplishments came at a cost for Bhutto. On November 3, 1993, her brother, Mir, returned to Pakistan from his exile in Syria. He intended to enter politics and become a rival to his sister for head of the PPP. Mir had become openly critical of his sister's policies. He felt that her husband had too much control over her.

As the family's oldest son, Mir was seen as the logical successor to his father—despite all that Bhutto had done for the PPP. Also, Mir had the support of Bhutto's mother. She had long been a vice-chair of the PPP. Bhutto dismissed her over her support of Mir. This caused tremendous bitterness within the Bhutto family.[6]

DOING THINGS HER WAY

Benazir Bhutto also became increasingly dictatorial in the way she ran Pakistan's government. Instead of having the National Assembly vote on new laws, she preferred to have President Leghari simply issue orders. In some ways, this was easier and less complicated. But she angered many when she tried to force through nominations to the country's

Charges of corruption

Throughout the 1990s, Benazir Bhutto and her husband, Asif Ali Zardari, were accused of improperly taking money. In 1999 they were convicted of corruption by the Lahore High Court. Some of the most damning evidence came from overseas. A Swiss court showed that Bhutto had bought a $175,000 necklace using money from an illegal bank account. However, the conviction was overturned. Later evidence showed that the trial had been fixed by Bhutto's political enemies.[7]

Bhutto's policy was to deny all charges of corruption. But in one high-profile case, she was shown to be either lying or badly fooled by her husband. In 1996 Zardari was accused of buying a mansion in Surrey, England, with money obtained corruptly. Both he and Bhutto ridiculed the idea. "How can anyone think of buying a mansion in England when people in Pakistan don't even have a roof over their heads?" Zardari once asked.[8]

However, in 2004, court documents would show that Zardari had in fact bought the house. This embarrassing news threw into doubt all of Bhutto's other denials of criminal activity. Those denials included matters of corruption and involvement in her brother's murder. Zardari would spend eight years in prison on various corruption charges.[9]

Supreme Court. Finally, Leghari was forced to make her withdraw the nominations. Nobody else supported them. This fight strained relations between her and the president.

FIGHTING SCANDALS

Bhutto and her husband also faced new accusations about corruption (see box). News broke that they had purchased a luxurious villa in Surrey,

This picture shows Benazir Bhutto in court in Karachi, Pakistan, 1997. At this point she had been dismissed as prime minister and was involved in fighting the various charges that had been brought against her.

England, with stolen government money. Bhutto was also accused of trying to buy votes of politicians from Punjab province. Opponents said she did it to make the government there friendlier to her.[10]

But it was another scandal—one involving her brother, Mir—that brought down Bhutto. On September 20, 1996, Mir and six other men were gunned down by police outside Mir's home in Karachi. The police said that they had simply tried to inspect his car. There had been several bombings in the area and such inspections were common. However, friends of Mir said that the police ambushed Mir and executed him.

A tribunal of three judges later found that Mir's death could not have taken place without approval from a "much higher" political authority. But the identity of that authority remained unclear. Bhutto seemed genuinely grieved at her brother's death. She and her mother were seen together barefoot, a sign of mourning in Pakistan.

But rumors soon circulated that Bhutto's husband, Asif Ali Zardari, had ordered Mir's assassination. (A 2008 court decision would later clear him of any charges.) True or not, that belief stuck in the public's mind. On November 4, 1996, President Leghari dismissed Bhutto as prime minister.[11] ❖

HEADLINES: 1997–2007

Here are some major news stories from the time of Bhutto's second exile.

Princess Diana Dies in Car Crash

Millions mourned after the UK's Princess Diana died in a car crash in Paris on August 31, 1997. There were theories that she had been murdered, but a public inquest in 2008 found no evidence to support this idea. Diana had a "fairy tale" wedding to Prince Charles in 1981, but their marriage ended in 1996.

President Clinton Impeached but Remains in Office

On December 19, 1998, U.S. President Bill Clinton became the second U.S. president to be impeached by the House of Representatives. This means that members of the House brought charges of misconduct against him, with the possibility of removing him from office if found guilty. However, the Senate voted against finding him guilty of the charges brought by the House. Clinton was accused of lying under oath in a personal matter.

Bush Narrowly Wins 2000 Presidential Race

In the fall of 2000, Republican George W. Bush defeated Democrat Al Gore to become U.S. president, even though Gore won more popular votes. Bush won a slim majority in the Electoral College, which decides the outcome of the presidential race.

Al Qaeda Terrorists Attack New York and Washington

On September 11, 2001, nearly 3,000 people died when Muslim hijackers crashed fuel-laden airplanes into the World Trade Center in New York City and the Pentagon in Washington, D.C. The terrorist attacks were funded and planned by al Qaeda leader Osama bin Laden.

The second hijacked plane, shown here moments before crashing into the second World Trade Center tower. Both towers collapsed shortly after being struck, due to the incredibly hot, burning jet fuel melting their internal supports.

U.S., Allies Invade Afghanistan

On October 7, 2001, the United States and several allies invaded Afghanistan. Their aim was to shut down the al Qaeda terrorist network, which had been responsible for the attacks of September 11. Al Qaeda had been given a place to stay by Afghanistan's fundamentalist Muslim leaders, known as the Taliban.

U.S. Invades Iraq

In March 2003, U.S. President George W. Bush directed U.S. troops to invade Iraq. U.S. leaders were convinced that Iraqi leader Saddam Hussein possessed weapons of mass destruction. However, no such weapons were found after the invasion.

Second Exile, Second Homecoming

Benazir Bhutto spent much of 1997 and 1998 fighting corruption charges. In 1999 she left Pakistan. She could not return without being imprisoned on corruption charges. In fact, her husband, Asif Ali Zardari, remained in prison until 2004.

During the late 1990s and early 2000s, Bhutto lived in exile in England and the United Arab Emirates (see map on page 15). She lived with her three children, Bilawal, Bakhtawar, and Asifa. "The [Pakistani] government waged relentless psychological warfare," she later said. "And it was very painful to have my reputation attacked. I lived in a state of uncertainty and anxiety. I never knew when I would be arrested at an airport [on charges of corruption]."[1]

On June 21, 2003, Bhutto reached her 50th birthday. She celebrated with about 100 friends at her residence in Dubai, a city in the United Arab Emirates. The guests at this party were given a pamphlet with a poem written by Bhutto. The poem was called "The Story of Benazir." One part of the poem read:

> I know I will return
> On a wave of the people's support
> Led by the bravest Party of them all
> A Party of martyrs
> A Party of struggle
> A Party that serves

Benazir Bhutto takes questions during a press conference.

> A Party of the people
> My enemies will wish I was never born
> For them it was a torture and a shame
> That I became
> The first woman leader of a Muslim state.[2]

During this time, she remained the head of the PPP. But many believed that her political career was over. She could not return to Pakistan, and her reputation had been soiled. She spent much of her time fighting the corruption charges in European and Pakistani courts. She denounced them in the press as being politically motivated.

STRAINED MARRIAGE

During this time, Bhutto's marriage to Zardari became strained. He spent 1998 to 2004 in prison, accused of corruption. In public, Bhutto defended him. She called him the "Mandela of Pakistan"—comparing him to Nelson Mandela, the legendary leader of South Africa who spent many years in prison under unjust charges (see page 58).[3]

In private, though, friends reported that the couple became distant. When Zardari was released from prison in 2004, he did not go to his family. Instead, he went to the United States for medical treatment for diabetes and other ailments. When he was called to court in London in 2006, he claimed to be suffering from mental illnesses, including depression. However, friends at the time said he was in good spirits.[4]

A TROUBLED COUNTRY

On February 17, 1997, Nawaz Sharif of the PML–N took over once again as prime minister. Once Bhutto left office, Pakistan—always a troubled country—became much more unstable politically. "Pakistan today is the most dangerous place in the world," wrote Bhutto in her final book, *Reconciliation: Islam, Democracy, and the West*. Most experts would agree.[5]

How did Pakistan become so much more dangerous? There are two main reasons. The first is its unique geography. On Pakistan's eastern border lies India. The tensions between India and Pakistan have boiled over into war three times since 1947. Both sides have nuclear weapons.

On Pakistan's western border lies Afghanistan (see map on page 15). In 1989 the Soviets pulled out of Afghanistan. They left chaos and civil war in their wake. In 1996 Afghanistan was taken over by the Taliban. The Taliban believed in an extreme fundamentalist version of Islam. The Taliban in turn gave shelter to the terrorist group al Qaeda.

Nuclear Pakistan

In the 1960s, India began trying to build nuclear weapons. News of this caused Pakistan to do the same. India tested its first nuclear weapon in 1974. By the mid-1980s, Pakistan had the ability to build one as well.

The Pakistanis held off on testing their own bomb, though. They did not want to upset other countries. However, that caution ended in 1998. That year India tested five nuclear weapons. Pakistan felt it had to respond, so it exploded its own weapons. Pakistan was officially a nuclear power. This upset many people. Pakistan is an unstable country. Muslim fundamentalists have a strong say in its government and military.[6]

GROWING TENSIONS

The second reason Pakistan has become dangerous is because of religious tensions. Since the time of Zia, conservative Muslims have tried to take Pakistan in a more fundamentalist direction. This is especially true of many tribal leaders who control the region near the border with Afghanistan. They want the country to be completely governed by Islamic laws.

More moderate people, like Bhutto, have tried to preserve a separation between religion and the government. This tension between the two sides has helped trigger international incidents. For instance, during Zia's regime, the government began training fundamentalist Muslims as terrorists to launch attacks in Kashmir (see box on page 17). Their bombings and other attacks have increased tensions with India.

In May 1999, Prime Minister Sharif led Pakistan into a disastrous border war with India. At one point there were fears that the war could **escalate** to the use of nuclear weapons. Within five months of this near disaster, he was overthrown in a military takeover. Pakistan was once again under military rule.[7]

THE RISE OF MUSHARRAF

On October 12, 1999, General Pervez Musharraf replaced Sharif as Pakistan's prime minister. Sharif had blamed Musharraf for starting the border war with India. Like Zia before him, Musharraf soon became an ally of the United States. The event that triggered that friendship was the September 11, 2001, terror attacks against the United States. The terror attacks had been masterminded by Osama bin Laden, the leader of al Qaeda, while he hid in Afghanistan. Pakistan helped the United States in its 2001 invasion of neighboring Afghanistan. The goal was to capture al Qaeda members and end the Taliban regime.

To stay in power, though, Musharraf had to walk a very thin tightrope. On the one hand, he took military aid from the United States to fight terrorism. On the other hand, he had to keep from angering powerful tribal leaders. They sided with the Taliban and al Qaeda. These tribal areas had been taken over by the very people the United States wanted to capture the most.[8]

But people within Pakistan were once again growing tired of military rule. Men in the military even stopped wearing their uniforms in the street because it provoked public anger. Meanwhile, the United States and European countries were pressuring Musharraf to restore democracy in Pakistan.[9]

RETURNING TO PAKISTAN

In October 2007, Bhutto struck a deal with General Musharraf. She and her husband would be allowed to return home. All corruption charges against them would be dropped. In exchange, Bhutto agreed to support Musharraf's reelection as president, an office he had assumed in 2006.[10]

Benazir Bhutto's return to Pakistan was marked by two violent bomb attacks. The attack was targeted at her motorcade, but ended up causing terrible harm to the crowd of Bhutto's supporters.

On October 18, 2007, Bhutto made a triumphant return to Pakistan. Once again, cheering crowds jammed the streets as her motorcade tried to pass. More than 150,000 people had come to welcome her.

However, her enemies were waiting for her as well. Suddenly a small bomb went off near her truck. It was almost immediately followed by a huge blast. The second explosion shattered windows in the truck that was carrying her. Fortunately, the truck was designed to withstand a bomb blast. As a result, no one inside was hurt.

The scene where the bombs had gone off was grim. Scores of people lay dead or bleeding and dying. Flames burned in the middle of the street. At least 130 people died in the two blasts. Everyone could tell this was a sign of things to come.[11] ❖

HEADLINES: 2007–2008

Here are some major news stories from the last years of Bhutto's life.

Final *Harry Potter* Book Released

In July 2007, the seventh and final book in the *Harry Potter* series appeared in bookstores. The series about the boy wizard, which began in 1997, was one of the best-selling book series of all time.

World Food Prices Spike

In January 2008, higher demand for food and a shorter supply caused food prices to soar worldwide. The higher prices were an inconvenience for shoppers in the United States and European countries. But the impact was much more severe in poorer countries. The shortage caused food riots and even toppled leaders in countries like Haiti.

Earthquake Kills 87,000 in China

On May 12, 2008, a massive earthquake struck central China, leaving 87,000 dead or missing. Another 5 million were left without homes.

Phelps Brings Home the Gold at the Beijing Olympics

U.S. swimmer Michael Phelps won a record eight gold medals at the 2008 Beijing Summer Olympics. Phelps surpassed the record of seven gold medals set by fellow U.S. swimmer Mark Spitz at the 1972 Olympics. China spent $44 billion on the games, almost four times the amount spent on the 2004 Summer Olympics in Athens, Greece.

Wall Street Plunges as Economy Collapses

Stock prices plunged in September 2008 after several large banks and companies failed. The U.S. government had to step in and bail out several companies to avoid a financial panic. The stock market collapse was part of a growing worldwide shortage of credit. The United States had entered a steep economic downturn in December 2007, as did several other countries. That made banks far less likely to lend money.

Barack Obama Wins U.S. Presidency

On November 4, 2008, Democrat Barack Obama defeated Republican John McCain to become the 44th president of the United States. Obama is the first African American chief executive.

Assassination

Benazir Bhutto tried to play it safe in the weeks after her return to Pakistan. She limited her public appearances. When she held political rallies, the crowds were deliberately small and easy to control. The time and place of each rally was always announced at the last minute. That prevented would-be assassins from planning an attack.[1]

However, Bhutto was a brave woman. In her 54 years, she had endured prison, illness, arrest, and dozens of attempts on her life. She had never backed down before the threat of physical harm. "I've adopted a philosophical view, and I don't dwell on threats," she once told an interviewer. "I feel that the time of my death is written; in that sense, I'm a fatalist [someone who accepts that events happen as they are meant to happen and are beyond one's control]."[2]

A DANGEROUS SITUATION

On December 27, 2007, Bhutto appeared at a rally in Rawalpindi, Pakistan. Unlike the previous rallies, journalists knew about it a week in advance. Photographs show Bhutto addressing a huge crowd. In typical fashion, Bhutto whipped up the crowd. Ironically, she spent most of her speech railing against terrorists within Pakistan. She said that Pakistan had to do a better job of fighting against them.[3]

Witnesses say that the problems began as Bhutto was getting ready to go. "When she left at the end of the rally, the crowd flocked out to the street and surrounded her car and danced and wanted to touch her," said John Moore, a photographer who was there. "It was very emotional."[4]

At that point, Bhutto made a fateful decision. The Land Cruiser SUV she was in had a sunroof. She opened it and rose up through it to wave good-bye. The people surrounding the car spotted her white scarf and went wild. They cheered and danced even more. But the car moved very slowly through the packed bodies. The driver could only lurch forward a few feet at a time.

Benazir Bhutto is shown here, greeting the crowd as she arrives at the December 27 campaign rally in 2007.

THE ASSASSIN STRIKES

As Bhutto rose through the sunroof of her SUV, the winter sun was falling quickly. Dusk had set in. But the celebration around Bhutto's car seemed ready to go on for hours. Just then, a clean-shaven man wearing sunglasses stepped forward. He raised a gun and shot three to five times at Bhutto. She quickly ducked down inside the bulletproof car for safety. But almost as soon as she did, a bomb went off near the left side of the car. There is evidence that there was a gunman and a suicide bomber.

People inside the SUV said that blood poured from wounds on Bhutto's head and neck. There was so much blood that a pool of it was found in the backseat. She lost consciousness and never regained it. Doctors later found that Bhutto died from a blow to the head. Perhaps she hit it while ducking from the bullets. Or perhaps the force of the bomb knocked her head into the sunroof.[5]

The SUV was too badly damaged to get Bhutto to Rawalpindi General Hospital. She had to be transferred to another vehicle to complete the journey. Surgeons at the hospital raced to save her life. But she was declared dead on the operating table.

GETTING THE TRAGIC NEWS

Thousands of PPP supporters gathered at the hospital to hear news of her condition. A hospital spokesman emerged to tell the crowd the bad news. The people who gathered roared with anger and disbelief. Some went on a rampage. They smashed the hospital's glass doors. Many people demanded to see the body as proof.

Meanwhile, ambulances arrived with more victims of the bombing attack. The explosion devastated the closely packed crowd. As the smoke cleared, people could see a gruesome tangle of dead bodies, shattered bicycles, shoes, clothes, and bloody campaign signs. At least 20 people died.[6]

Many of Bhutto's supporters could not believe that their leader was dead. "Today there is no more Pakistan," cried Sher Zaman, one of Bhutto's supporters. Tears streamed down his cheeks. "The woman who has defended us has died. I'm seventy years old, but today I feel like an orphan."[7]

Before she died, Bhutto and her supporters said that President Musharraf did not provide her with enough security. Her assassin, though, was probably sent by a pro-Taliban tribal leader named Baitullah Mehsud. He lived in a region near the Afghan border. He was one of the tribal leaders who had made that area of Pakistan such a lawless region.[8]

"BHUTTO LIVES!"

Three days later, the PPP members gathered. They wept and chanted "Bhutto lives!" They also honored the wishes left in her will. That included naming her 19-year-old son, Bilawal, as the party's leader. However, Bilawal was still too young to actually run the party. So his father, Asif Ali Zardari, became leader of the PPP. He acted on behalf of Bilawal, who went back to school at Oxford.[9]

Zardari's rise to power disturbed many both inside and outside Pakistan. Bhutto's closest aides blamed his corruption for bringing down both of her governments. For the same reason, many ordinary Pakistanis did not trust him. His previous claims to suffer from mental problems (see page 82) worried foreign governments. They were concerned that he might soon control Pakistan's nuclear weapons.[10]

Despite all this, Zardari became the PPP's leader. On February 18, 2008, Zardari led the party to victory in the National Assembly. The PPP won by forming a coalition with Bhutto's old rival, Nawaz Sharif, and Sharif's PML–N. Then on September 6, 2008, Zardari won enough votes from the National Assembly and regional assemblies to become president of Pakistan. Zardari had finished the comeback that Bhutto had begun in October 2007.[11]

Benazir Bhutto's son, Bilawal, in January, 2008.

NOT FORGOTTEN

Bhutto may be gone. But Pakistanis still honor her memory, just as they do the memory of her father. On December 27, 2008—the first anniversary of Bhutto's death—more than 150,000 Pakistanis flocked to her gravesite. She was buried at the family mausoleum at Garhi Khuda Bakhsh, a village in Sindh province. Some people had walked hundreds of miles. They wanted to offer flowers and kiss her grave. Many of them beat their heads and chests in a sign of mourning.

Bhutto left behind a troubled country of 152 million people. It is gripped by a high jobless rate and a rising tide of terrorist violence. In fact, those behind Bhutto's murder have not yet been brought to justice. But people love her even after she is gone because she was a beacon of hope. "She gave her life for the people of this country," said Sher Mohammad, 23, whose feet were swollen from his journey on foot to her mausoleum. "So we can walk a few miles to pay homage to her dignity."[12] ❖

Timeline

1947   INDIA AND PAKISTAN BECOME INDEPENDENT FROM GREAT BRITAIN. RELIGIOUS FIGHTING BETWEEN MUSLIMS AND HINDUS KILLS AT LEAST 500,000. ANOTHER 14 MILLION ARE DRIVEN FROM THEIR HOMES. MOST MUSLIMS GO TO PAKISTAN; HINDUS TO INDIA.

1953   Benazir Bhutto is born in Karachi, Pakistan.

1963   Benazir Bhutto sent to Catholic boarding school in Murree, Pakistan.

        U.S. PRESIDENT JOHN F. KENNEDY IS ASSASSINATED.

1965   WAR BREAKS OUT BETWEEN INDIA AND PAKISTAN OVER THE KASHMIR REGION.

1967   Zulfikar Bhutto founds the Pakistan People's Party (PPP).

        ARAB NATIONS AND ISRAEL FIGHT THE SIX-DAY WAR. ISRAEL MAKES LARGE TERRITORIAL GAINS, INCLUDING THE CITY OF JERUSALEM. THIS IS A HUGE BLOW TO ARAB AND MUSLIM PRIDE.

1969   Benazir Bhutto arrives at Radcliffe College (now part of Harvard) in Cambridge, Massachusetts.

1971   CIVIL WAR BETWEEN EAST PAKISTAN AND WEST PAKISTAN CAUSES BLOODY FIGHTING. INDIA TAKES THE SIDE OF EAST PAKISTAN. EAST PAKISTAN BECOMES THE INDEPENDENT COUNTRY OF BANGLADESH. WEST PAKISTAN BECOMES PAKISTAN.

        Zulfikar Bhutto becomes prime minister and later president of Pakistan.

1973   Benazir Bhutto graduates from Radcliffe and begins attending the University of Oxford in England.

1976   Benazir Bhutto becomes first Asian woman to become president of the Oxford Union Debating Society.

1977   Benazir Bhutto returns home to Pakistan.

A military coup led by General Muhammad Zia ul-Haq overthrows Zulfikar Bhutto and places him under arrest.

1979   Zia's regime executes Zulfikar Bhutto. Benazir Bhutto spends most of the next five years in prison or under house arrest.

SHAH OF IRAN IS OVERTHROWN. HE IS REPLACED BY RADICAL MUSLIM RULERS.

CAMP DAVID PEACE TALKS BRING PEACE BETWEEN ISRAEL AND EGYPT. THIS PEACE ANGERS MUSLIM EXTREMISTS.

RADICAL MUSLIM STUDENTS TAKE OVER THE U.S. EMBASSY IN TEHRAN, IRAN, AND HOLD HOSTAGES FOR 444 DAYS WITH THE APPROVAL OF THE IRANIAN GOVERNMENT.

A GROUP OF ABOUT 500 RADICAL MUSLIMS TAKES OVER THE GRAND MOSQUE IN MECCA, SAUDI ARABIA, THE HOLIEST SITE IN ISLAM. THE FIGHTING LASTS FOR TWO WEEKS AND KILLS AT LEAST 4,000 PEOPLE.

SOVIET UNION INVADES AFGHANISTAN, CAUSING TENS OF THOUSANDS OF REFUGEES TO FLEE TO PAKISTAN.

MARGARET THATCHER IS ELECTED PRIME MINISTER OF THE UNITED KINGDOM.

1980   WAR BREAKS OUT BETWEEN IRAN AND IRAQ. IT LASTS EIGHT YEARS AND KILLS AT LEAST 400,000.

RONALD REAGAN IS ELECTED U.S. PRESIDENT.

1983   A SUICIDE BOMBER DRIVES A TRUCK FULL OF EXPLOSIVES INTO A MARINE BASE IN LEBANON. THE EXPLOSION KILLS 241 AND PROMPTS THE UNITED STATES TO PULL ITS TROOPS OUT OF LEBANON.

1984   Bhutto is allowed to leave Pakistan to seek medical treatment for a serious ear ailment.

1985   Bhutto's brother Shah dies mysteriously in France. Huge crowds gather when his body is brought back to Pakistan.

1986   Bhutto gets a hero's welcome when she returns to Pakistan. Thousands line the streets to greet her.

THE CHERNOBYL NUCLEAR ACCIDENT IN THE SOVIET UNION KILLS AT LEAST 4,000 AND CONTAMINATES A VAST AREA WITH RADIATION.

1987   Bhutto marries Asif Ali Zardari.

1988   General Zia dies in a mysterious plane crash. Bhutto gives birth to the first of her three children during her campaign to be elected prime minister. She wins the election, becoming Pakistan's first female leader.

GEORGE H.W. BUSH IS ELECTED U.S. PRESIDENT.

1989   THE BERLIN WALL FALLS. COMMUNIST COUNTRIES IN EASTERN EUROPE BEGIN TO FALL.

1990   NELSON MANDELA IS RELEASED FROM A SOUTH AFRICAN PRISON AFTER 27 YEARS.

IRAQ INVADES KUWAIT, TRIGGERING THE GULF WAR.

President Ishaq removes Bhutto from office before her term ends. She leaves office amid allegations of corruption against her and her husband.

1991   THE SOVIET UNION COLLAPSES, ENDING THE WORLD'S LARGEST AND MOST POWERFUL COMMUNIST GOVERNMENT.

1992   BILL CLINTON IS ELECTED U.S. PRESIDENT.

1993   Bhutto is once again elected prime minister.

1996   Bhutto's brother Mir is gunned down in Pakistan under mysterious circumstances.

Bhutto is again forced from office amid allegations of corruption.

1997	Bhutto's husband is imprisoned on corruption charges (he remains in prison until 2004). Bhutto lives overseas to avoid prosecution.

TONY BLAIR ELECTED PRIME MINISTER OF THE UNITED KINGDOM.

2000   GEORGE W. BUSH WINS A CONTROVERSIAL ELECTION TO BECOME U.S. PRESIDENT.

2001   ON SEPTEMBER 11, THREE U.S. AIRPLANES ARE HIJACKED AND FLOWN INTO THE WORLD TRADE CENTER IN NEW YORK AND THE PENTAGON IN WASHINGTON. A FOURTH HIJACKED PLANE CRASHES IN PENNSYLVANIA, APPARENTLY ON ITS WAY TO THE U.S. CAPITOL.

THE U.S. INVADES AFGHANISTAN, WHERE THE SEPTEMBER 11 ATTACK ORIGINATED. THE ATTACK'S MASTERMIND, OSAMA BIN LADEN, ESCAPES. HE IS BELIEVED TO HAVE FLED INTO PAKISTAN.

2007   GORDON BROWN BECOMES PRIME MINISTER OF THE UNITED KINGDOM.

Bhutto makes a deal with Pakistan's leader, General Musharraf. All corruption charges are dropped against her and her husband. She supports Musharraf for president.

Bhutto returns to Pakistan and survives one serious assassination attempt.

A second assassination attempt on December 27 is successful. Benazir Bhutto dies.

WORLD ECONOMY ENTERS A STEEP DOWNTURN, CAUSING MILLIONS OF PEOPLE TO LOSE THEIR JOBS.

2008   Bhutto's husband becomes president of Pakistan.

BARAK OBAMA IS ELECTED U.S. PRESIDENT.

Glossary

Arab member of a group of people originally from the Arabian peninsula and neighboring areas. Arabs now live in most of the Middle East and North Africa.

atheist person who does not believe in God

censorship examining and preventing the distribution of books, movies, or other media that are found to be offensive or politically unacceptable

civil war war between two organized groups for control of the same country or region, or to change a government policy

civilian person who is not in the armed forces or the police

coalition group in which different groups or people agree to work toward the same goal

Cold War mostly nonviolent—or "cold"—war that pitted the United States and its allies against the Soviet Union and its allies. It lasted from 1946 to 1991.

colony country or region that is under the control of another country or region

communist person or government that believes the government should own all property. In practice, this belief often leads to great limits on personal freedom.

corruption dishonest behavior by those in power, usually involving a desire for money

democracy government system in which all people have a say in how the government is run

dictator absolute ruler who holds power without elections

escalate to cause something to increase in intensity

ethnic group group of people who identify with each other and have a common history. Such groups often share the same language, values, and religious beliefs.

exile being barred from living in one's home country

fundamentalist person who strictly follows any set of beliefs

Hindu person who follows the ancient religion of Hinduism, which is practiced mostly in India. Hindus worship many gods and goddesses.

human rights rights believed to belong to all people, such as freedom of speech, the right to a fair trial, and so on

insurgent person who rebels against existing leaders, often violently and in secret

Islam religion focused on the worship of God, as revealed by the Prophet Muhammad in the 600s CE. Its followers are found mostly in Asia, North Africa, and the Middle East.

martial law law that is imposed by government or military forces when normal law and order has broken down

Muslim follower of Islam

National Assembly Pakistan's parliament, or lawmaking body

Pakistan Muslim League–Nawaz (PML–N) Pakistani political party led by Nawaz Sharif. Sharif committed to making Pakistan a more firmly Muslim country.

Pakistan National Alliance (PNA) alliance of nine mostly conservative parties that banded together against the PPP in Pakistan's 1977 election

Pakistan People's Party (PPP) Pakistani political party founded by Zulfikar Bhutto, the father of Benazir Bhutto. It is committed to helping the poor and making Pakistan more democratic.

reform change made in order to improve something

regime government, usually a nondemocratic one

repression act of forcefully restricting something, such as people's freedoms

Sharia body of laws based largely on the Koran (Qur'an), the holy book of Islam, the sayings and traditions of the Prophet Muhammad, and rulings by Islamic scholars

solitary confinement form of imprisonment that involves little or no contact with any other people

Soviet Union former group of communist republics that had its capital in Moscow. Russia was the largest and most dominant member of the Soviet Union.

Taliban government set up by fundamentalist Muslims in Afghanistan in the early 1990s

United Nations (U.N.) group of countries that joined together in 1945 to promote world peace and international cooperation

Notes on Sources

COMING TO POWER (PAGES 6–9)

1. Owen Bennett Jones, *Pakistan: Eye of the Storm* (New Haven, Conn.: Yale University Press, 2002), 230.

2. Christophe Jaffrelot, ed., *A History of Pakistan and Its Origins* (New York: Anthem, 2002), 83–85.

3. Barbara Crossette, "Bhutto Pledges to Aid Women, Students, Labor," *New York Times*, December 3, 1988.

4. Benazir Bhutto, *Daughter of Destiny: An Autobiography* (New York: Simon and Schuster, 1989), 33, 42.

GROWING UP (PAGES 12–19)

1. Bhutto, *Daughter of Destiny*, 33, 42; Katherine M. Doherty and Craig A. Doherty, *Benazir Bhutto* (New York: Franklin Watts, 1990), 37–39.

2. Bhutto, *Daughter of Destiny*, 43.

3. Doherty and Doherty, *Benazir Bhutto*, 38.

4. Bhutto, *Daughter of Destiny*, 44.

5. Mark Weston, *The Land and People of Pakistan* (New York: HarperCollins, 1992), 90; www.bbc.co.uk/worldservice/learningenglish/communicate/blog/student/0000009647. shtml.

6. "India–Pakistan: Troubled Relations: Partition and Independence," *BBC News*, http://news.bbc.co.uk/hi/english/static/in_depth/south_asia/2002/india_pakistan/ timeline/1947.stm.

7. Bhutto, *Daughter of Destiny*, 42; Doherty and Doherty, *Benazir Bhutto*, 25.

8. Bhutto, *Daughter of Destiny*, 43; Doherty and Doherty, *Benazir Bhutto*, 28.

9. Bhutto, *Daughter of Destiny*, 43; Doherty and Doherty, *Benazir Bhutto*, 38.

10. Bhutto, *Daughter of Destiny*, 43–44.

11. Bhutto, *Daughter of Destiny*, 46–47.

12. Bhutto, *Daughter of Destiny*, 47.

13. Bhutto, *Daughter of Destiny*, 48; Libby Hughes, *Benazir Bhutto: From Prison to Prime Minister* (Minneapolis: Dillon, 1990), 16.

14. "Quick Guide: Kashmir Dispute," *BBC News*, http://news.bbc.co.uk/2/hi/south_asia/5030514.stm.

15. Bhutto, *Daughter of Destiny*, 48; Doherty and Doherty, *Benazir Bhutto*, 40; Hughes, *From Prison to Prime Minister*, 16.

16. Bhutto, *Daughter of Destiny*, 49–51.

17. Weston, *Land and People*, 105.

18. Bhutto, *Daughter of Destiny*, 50–51.

19. Bhutto, *Daughter of Destiny*, 51.

20. Doherty and Doherty, *Benazir Bhutto*, 40; Hughes, *From Prison to Prime Minister*, 17–18.

21. Weston, *Land and People*, 136–54; "Profile: Asif Ali Zardari," *Times of London*, September 7, 2008.

THE HAPPIEST YEARS (PAGES 22–29)

1. Bhutto, *Daughter of Destiny*, 54–55.

2. Bhutto, *Daughter of Destiny*, 58, 82.

3. Bhutto, *Daughter of Destiny*, 58–59.

4. Doherty and Doherty, *Benazir Bhutto*, 41.

5. Bhutto, *Daughter of Destiny*, 54–55.

6. Bhutto, *Daughter of Destiny*, 58–59; Doherty and Doherty, *Benazir Bhutto*, 41.

7. Bhutto, *Daughter of Destiny*, 59.

8. Bhutto, *Daughter of Destiny*, 60.

9. "1967: Thousands Join Anti-War Movement," *BBC News*, http://news.bbc.co.uk/onthisday/hi/dates/stories/october/20/newsid_3153000/3153144.stm.

10. Bhutto, *Daughter of Destiny*, 63–65.

11. Bhutto, *Daughter of Destiny*, 69.

12. Bhutto, *Daughter of Destiny*, 69–72.

13. Bhutto, *Daughter of Destiny*, 75.

14. Bhutto, *Daughter of Destiny*, 79–83; Elections.com, "Pakistan Elections," http://www.elections.com.pk/candidatedetails.php?id=6877.

15. Doherty and Doherty, *Benazir Bhutto*, 48.

16. Jaffrelot, *History of Pakistan*, 50–59.

17. Bhutto, *Daughter of Destiny*, 86.

ZIA TAKES OVER (PAGES 32–41)

1. Bhutto, *Daughter of Destiny*, 93–94.

2. Weston, *Land and People*, 116.

3. Weston, *Land and People*, 110–13.

4. Weston, *Land and People*, 110–13.

5. Weston, *Land and People*, 116–23; StoryofPakistan.com, "General Muhammad Zia-ul-Haq (1924–88)," http://www.storyofpakistan.com/person.asp?perid=P020.

6. Bhutto, *Daughter of Destiny*, 98, 103.

7. Weston, *Land and People*, 116; Bennett Jones, *Eye of the Storm*, 227–30.

8. Bhutto, *Daughter of Destiny*, 101–5.

9. Doherty and Doherty, *Benazir Bhutto*, 50–51; Bhutto, *Daughter of Destiny*, 119–20.

10. Bhutto, *Daughter of Destiny*, 125.

11. Bhutto, *Daughter of Destiny*, 127.

12. Bennett Jones, *Eye of the Storm*, 227–30; Lawrence Ziring, *Pakistan at the Crosscurrent of History* (Oxford: OneWorld, 2003), 167–68.

13. Doherty and Doherty, *Benazir Bhutto*, 54.

14. Bhutto, *Daughter of Destiny*, 106–10.

15. Bhutto, *Daughter of Destiny*, 18, 163.

16. Bhutto, *Daughter of Destiny*, 22.

17. Bhutto, *Daughter of Destiny*, 18–23; Mary Anne Weaver, "Bhutto's Fateful Moment," *The New Yorker*, October 4, 1993, http://www.newyorker.com/archive/1993/10/04/1993_10_04_082_TNY_CARDS_000365108?currentPage=all.

18. Doherty and Doherty, *Benazir Bhutto*, 64–65.

19. Jaffrelot, *History of Pakistan*, 79–80; Robert G. Wirsing, *Pakistan's Security Under Zia: The Policy Imperatives of a Peripheral Asian State* (New York: St. Martin's, 1991), 197; Countrystudies.us, "Pakistan," http://countrystudies.us/pakistan/21.htm.

20. Bhutto, *Daughter of Destiny*, 174–75.

YEARS OF SUFFERING (PAGES 44–47)

1. Weaver, "Bhutto's Fateful Moment."

2. Doherty and Doherty, *Benazir Bhutto*, 65.

3. Bhutto, *Daughter of Destiny*, 179–83.

4. Bhutto, *Daughter of Destiny*, 179–83.

5. Bhutto, *Daughter of Destiny*, 200; Weaver, "Bhutto's Fateful Moment."

6. Bhutto, *Daughter of Destiny*, 189–99.

7. Bhutto, *Daughter of Destiny*, 214–22.

8. Bhutto, *Daughter of Destiny*, 78–79, 210, 239, 243–45, 250–51, 260–61; Doherty and Doherty, *Benazir Bhutto*, 71; American Speech-Language-Hearing Association, "How Hearing and Balance Work," http://www.asha.org/public/hearing/anatomy/.

9. Bhutto, *Daughter of Destiny*, 250–53; Doherty and Doherty, *Benazir Bhutto*, 73–74.

EXILE AND RETURN (PAGES 50–57)

1. Bhutto, *Daughter of Destiny*, 261.

2. Bhutto, *Daughter of Destiny*, 259.

3. Bhutto, *Daughter of Destiny*, 259.

4. Bhutto, *Daughter of Destiny*, 258.

5. Bhutto, *Daughter of Destiny*, 258–59, 274.

6. Hughes, *From Prison to Prime Minister*, 84–86.

7. Hughes, *From Prison to Prime Minister*, 84–86.

8. Bhutto, *Daughter of Destiny*, 292–302.

9. Bhutto, *Daughter of Destiny*, 300; Benazir Bhutto, *Reconciliation: Islam, Democracy, and the West* (New York: HarperCollins, 2008), 190–91.

10. Bhutto, *Daughter of Destiny*, 300–11.

11. Bhutto, *Daughter of Destiny*, 322–26.

12. Bhutto, *Daughter of Destiny*, 329.

13. Hughes, *From Prison to Prime Minister*, 100–1.

14. Bhutto, *Daughter of Destiny*, 350–65; Doherty and Doherty, *Benazir Bhutto*, 103–10.

SUDDEN VICTORY, SUDDEN DEFEAT (PAGES 60–69)

1. Bhutto, *Reconciliation*, 191.

2. Bhutto, *Reconciliation*, 192; Doherty and Doherty, *Benazir Bhutto*, 112.

3. Bhutto, *Reconciliation*, 192.

4. Weston, *Land and People*, 116–23; StoryofPakistan.com, "General Muhammad Zia-ul-Haq (1924–88)."

5. Bhutto, *Daughter of Destiny*, 379.

6. Bhutto, *Daughter of Destiny*, 86–87.

7. Bhutto, *Daughter of Destiny*, 389, 392–95.

8. Jaffrelot, *History of Pakistan*, 83–84; Weaver, "Bhutto's Fateful Moment."

9. E. A. Wayne, "An Interview with Benazir Bhutto," *Christian Science Monitor*, May 31, 1988.

10. Bhutto, *Reconciliation*, 199.

11. Adnan Adil, "Pakistan Women's Rights Take Centre Stage," *BBC News*, November 11, 2003; Bhutto, *Daughter of Destiny*, 317; Jaffrelot, *History of Pakistan*, 248.

12. Weaver, "Bhutto's Fateful Moment"; Bhutto, *Reconciliation*, 203.

13. Weaver, "Bhutto's Fateful Moment."

14. Weaver, "Bhutto's Fateful Moment"; Bennett Jones, *Eye of the Storm*, 240.

15. Steven Coll, "Time Bomb: The Death of Benazir Bhutto and the Unraveling of Pakistan," *The New Yorker*, January 28, 2008, http://www.newyorker.com/reporting/2008/01/28/080128fa_fact_coll.

16. Jaffrelot, *History of Pakistan*, 84; Weston, *Land and People*, 10.

17. Central Intelligence Agency, "The World Factbook: Pakistan," https://www.cia.gov/library/publications/the-world-factbook/geos/pk.html.

18. Jaffrelot, *History of Pakistan*, 33–36.

19. Weaver, "Bhutto's Fateful Moment."

20. Weston, *Land and People*, 128; Ziring, *Crosscurrent of History*, 215.

21. Ziring, *Crosscurrent of History*, 216; Jaffrelot, *History of Pakistan*, 292.

PRIME MINISTER AGAIN (PAGES 72–77)

1. Weaver, "Bhutto's Fateful Moment."
2. Jaffrelot, *History of Pakistan*, 292–93; Weaver, "Bhutto's Fateful Moment."
3. Jaffrelot, *History of Pakistan*, 86; Bhutto, *Reconciliation*, 204.
4. Weaver, "Bhutto's Fateful Moment."
5. Jaffrelot, *History of Pakistan*, 86–89, 293; Bhutto, *Reconciliation*, 207.
6. Ziring, *Crosscurrent of History*, 241–42; Jaffrelot, *History of Pakistan*, 87–88.
7. Bennett Jones, *Eye of the Storm*, 234–35.
8. Hasan Suroor, "New Turn in 'Mansion' Controversy," *The Hindu*, August 21, 2004.
9. Bennett Jones, *Eye of the Storm*, 234–35; Suroor, "New Turn."
10. Jaffrelot, *History of Pakistan*, 87–88; "Zardari Surprise Admission to Surrey Palace Ownership," *Pakistan Times*, August 18, 2004.
11. Jaffrelot, *History of Pakistan*, 87–88; Razzak Abro, "Death Anniversary of Murtaza Bhutto Today," *Daily Times*, September 20, 2008.

SECOND EXILE, SECOND HOMECOMING (PAGES 80–85)

1. Coll, "Time Bomb."
2. "A Former Prime Minister Invokes the Muse," *Daily Times*, June 21, 2003.
3. Coll, "Time Bomb."
4. "Profile: Asif Ali Zardari."
5. Bhutto, *Reconciliation*, 210.
6. Weston, *Land and People*, 114–15; "Timeline: Pakistan," BBC News, http://news.bbc.co.uk/2/hi/south_asia/country_profiles/1156716.stm; Bennett Jones, *Eye of the Storm*, 187–222.
7. Bhutto, *Reconciliation*, 209–12; Coll, "Time Bomb."
8. Council on Foreign Relations, "A Conversation with Benazir Bhutto," transcript, August 15, 2007; "Profile: Asif Ali Zardari."
9. Council on Foreign Relations, "A Conversation with Benazir Bhutto."
10. Coll, "Time Bomb."
11. "Attack on Bhutto Convoy Kills 130," *BBC News*, October 19, 2007, http://news.bbc.co.uk/2/hi/south_asia/7051804.stm; Jawa Report, "Al-Qaeda Assassination Attempt on Bhutto," October 19, 2007, http://mypetjawa.mu.nu/archives/189816.php.

ASSASSINATION (PAGES 88–93)

1. John Moore, interview, *New York Times*, http://www.nytimes.com/packages/html/world/20071227_BHUTTO_FEATURE/.
2. Weaver, "Bhutto's Fateful Moment."

3. John Moore, interview; Griff Witte, "Bhutto Assassination Sparks Chaos," *Washington Post*, December 28, 2007; "Q&A: Benazir Bhutto Assassination," *BBC News*, http://news.bbc.co.uk/2/hi/south_asia/6653475.stm.

4. John Moore, interview.

5. John Moore, interview; Witte, "Bhutto Assassination Sparks Chaos"; Coll, "Time Bomb"; "Documents: Medical Examiners' Report on Benazir Bhutto," *Washingtonpost. com*,

http://www.washingtonpost.com/wp-srv/world/articles/bhutto_medicalreport_010108.html.

6. John Moore, interview; Witte, "Bhutto Assassination Sparks Chaos."

7. Witte, "Bhutto Assassination Sparks Chaos."

8. Syed Shoaib Hasan, "Profile: Baitullah Mehsud," *BBC News*, December 29, 2007, http://news.bbc.co.uk/2/hi/south_asia/7163626.stm.

9. Associated Press, "Bhutto's Husband Haunted by a Past of Corruption Allegations," December 30, 2007.

10. "Profile: Asif Ali Zardari"; Coll, "Time Bomb."

11. Carlotta Gall, "Bhutto Spouse, Divisive Figure, Asserts Himself," *New York Times*, January 1, 2008; Jane Perlez, "From Prison to Zenith of Politics in Pakistan," *New York Times*, March 11, 2008; Jane Perlez, "Bhutto's Widower, Viewed as Ally by U.S., Wins the Pakistani Presidency Handily," *New York Times*, September 7, 2008.

12. Associated Press, "Crowds in Pakistan Mark Bhutto's Death," December 27, 2008.

Further Reading

Bennett Jones, Owen. *Pakistan: Eye of the Storm*. New Haven, Conn.: Yale University Press, 2002.

Bhutto, Benazir. *Daughter of Destiny: An Autobiography*. New York: Simon and Schuster, 1989.

Bhutto, Benazir. *Reconciliation: Islam, Democracy, and the West*. New York: HarperCollins, 2008.

Coll, Steve. *Ghost Wars: The Secret History of the CIA, Afghanistan, and bin Laden, from the Soviet Invasion to September 10, 2001*. New York: Penguin, 2004.

Corbin, Jane. *Al-Qaeda: In Search of the Terror Network that Threatens the World*. New York: Thunder's Mouth Press, 2002.

Doherty, Katherine M., and Doherty, Craig A. *Benazir Bhutto*. New York: Franklin Watts, 1990.

Hughes, Libby. *Benazir Bhutto: From Prison to Prime Minister*. Minneapolis, Minn.: Dillon Press, 1990.

Hussain, Zahid. *Frontline Pakistan: The Struggle with Militant Islam*. New York: Columbia University, 2008.

Jaffrelot, Christophe, ed. *A History of Pakistan and Its Origins*. New York: Anthem Press, 2002.

Khan, Yasmin. *The Great Partition: The Making of India and Pakistan*. New Haven, Conn.: Yale University Press, 2008.

Khan, Yasmin. *The Great Partition: The Making of India and Pakistan.* New Haven, Conn.: Yale University Press, 2008.

Leeming, Matthew, and Omrani, Bijan. *Afghanistan: A Companion and Guide.* New York: Odyssey, 2005.

Nawaz, Shuja. *Crossed Swords: Pakistan, Its Army, and the Wars Within.* New York: Oxford University, 2008.

Rashid, Ahmed. *Taliban: Militant Islam, Oil and Fundamentalism in Central Asia.* New Haven, Conn.: Yale Nota Bene, 2001.

Rashid, Ahmed. *Descent into Chaos: The U.S. and the Disaster in Pakistan, Afghanistan, and Central Asia.* New York: Penguin, 2009.

Weston, Mark. *The Land and People of Pakistan.* New York: HarperCollins, 1992.

Wirsing, Robert G. *Pakistan's Security Under Zia: The Policy Imperatives of a Peripheral Asian State.* New York: St. Martin's Press, 1991.

Wright, Lawrence. *The Looming Tower: Al-Qaeda and the Road to 9/11.* New York, Vintage, 2006.

Ziring, Lawrence. *Pakistan at the Crosscurrent of History.* Oxford, England: OneWorld, 2003.

Find Out More

http://www.benazirbhutto.org/

> *Benazir Bhutto's official website provides a wide array of resources, including a profile and links to articles that have been written about her.*

http://news.bbc.co.uk/2/hi/south_asia/2228796.stm

> *This BBC profile on Bhutto after her assassination summarizes her life and accomplishments. It also provides links to related articles on Pakistani life and politics.*

http://www.time.com/time/photogallery/0,29307,1698497,00.html

> *This TIME magazine photo gallery shows Bhutto's "life in pictures," providing insight into the many factors that influenced her life.*

http://www.csmonitor.com/2007/1228/p25s04-wosc.html

> *This 1988 Christian Science Monitor interview with Bhutto explains the many obstacles she faced as she rose to power. It also reflects the issues and attitudes that were prevalent at the time.*

http://www.aol.in/news/gallery/bhutto_diary_07/1/false/6000/gallery.jhtml

> *This AOL photo gallery shows Bhutto's life in pictures. It mixes private family-oriented photos with Bhutto in action as a politician and leader of Pakistan.*

http://www.newyorker.com/archive/1993/10/04/1993_10_04_082_TNY_CARDS_000365108?currentPage=all

> *This New Yorker magazine profile on Benazir Bhutto from 1993 provides a thorough review of her life up to that point. It also helps explain the political situation in Pakistan.*

https://www.cia.gov/library/publications/the-world-factbook/geos/pk.html

> *The CIA Fact Book contains important vital statistics and background on Pakistan. Those statistics cover areas such as geography, economy, and population.*

http://news.bbc.co.uk/2/hi/south_asia/country_profiles/1156716.stm

> *This BBC timeline of Pakistan's history helps explain the country's turbulent history and Bhutto's place in it.*

http://news.bbc.co.uk/2/hi/south_asia/country_profiles/1157960.stm

> *This BBC country profile provides a brief overview of Pakistan's history. It also provides links to vital statistics and other background material.*

http://www.cfr.org/publication/14041/

This Council on Foreign Relations interview with Bhutto from 2007 helps explain her attitudes toward Pakistan and her reasons for wanting to become the country's leader once again.

http://www.nytimes.com/packages/html/world/20071227_BHUTTO_FEATURE/

This audio interview of photographer John Moore gives a moment-by-moment description of Bhutto's assassination. It also shows what a typical Bhutto rally was like.

http://www.arabianbusiness.com/index2.php?option=com_gallery&id=542141

This photo gallery from ArabianBuisiness.com shows the many ways that Pakistani people mourned Bhutto's death.

http://www.pbs.org/wgbh/pages/frontline/shows/front/

This companion website to the PBS documentary "Al Qaeda's New Front" shows the efforts al Qaeda has made since September 11, 2001, to bring its message of radical Islam to Pakistan and the Middle East.

http://www.newyorker.com/reporting/2008/01/28/080128fa_fact_coll

This New Yorker *magazine article by journalist Stephen Coll explains how Bhutto's assassination happened and the impact it is likely to have on Pakistan and the rest of the world.*

http://www.nytimes.com/2009/04/05/magazine/05zardari-t.html?pagewanted=1&n=Top/News/World/Countries%20and%20Territories/Pakistan

This New York Times Magazine *article explains the personality of Bhutto's husband Asif Zardari and the challenges that await him as president of Pakistan.*

http://news.bbc.co.uk/2/hi/south_asia/4032997.stm

This BBC profile on Zardari provides background into his past, including the many corruption scandals that have surrounded him.

http://www.timesonline.co.uk/tol/news/world/asia/article4692223.ece

This Times of London *profile on Zardari helps explain his personality and the many criticisms that have been leveled against him as Bhutto's husband and as a politician.*

Index